Ghost-Hunter's Casebook

To Janie, for unstinting help and support.

Ghost-Hunter's Casebook

―――⟫◆⟪―――

The Investigations of Andrew Green Revisited

Bowen Pearse

TEMPUS

to expect from this book

All entries have been newly researched and the best brought up to date. The nucleus of each entry remains, but because some thirty or forty years have elapsed since the works were originally published, often only a sentence or two of Andrew's original remains. Some ninety per cent is entirely new material, researched and written in the two years proceeding publication.

About the author

Bowen Pearse was born and brought up on a cattle station in the Hunter Valley in Australia. His first job was with a Sydney advertising agency – to write copy in 'language the countryman understands'. He then travelled extensively in Asia and Europe, and worked as a copywriter and journalist in Hong Kong, Tokyo and London, before qualifying as a librarian, specialising in local history. He now lives in the country in a sixteenth-century Kentish farmhouse.

First published 2007

Tempus Publishing
Cirencester Road, Chalford
Stroud, Gloucestershire, GL6 8PE
www.tempus-publishing.com

Tempus Publishing is an imprint of NPI Media Group

British Library Cataloguing in Publication Data.
A catalogue record for this book is available from the British Library.

ISBN 978 0 7524 4500 7

Typesetting and origination by NPI Media Group
Printed and bound in Great Britain

Contents

Acknowledgements

My special thanks to Norah, Andrew's widow, who graciously gave me full access to all Andrew's files and was never tired by my constant phone calls for this or that concerning Andrew's life. Thanks too to Chris McCooey and Alan Murdie for also reading the MS, both bringing their own special talents to work. My thanks also to Jeremy Passmore who helped especially in queries over history. It goes without saying that Kent librarians managed to get me every obscure title, and fielded every question bowled at them. I am also indebted to Daryl Burchmore for introducing me to Pluckley, Kent's haunted village. My especial thanks to Michael Kenny for some of the most amazing ghost stories. And also to all the contributors at each ghostly site who so patiently answered all my endless queries.

Foreword

BY ALAN MURDIE

It is with a mixture of both pleasure and sadness that I write an introduction to Bowen Pearse's book *Ghost-Hunter's Case Book: Investigations of Andrew Green Revisited*. The pleasure is in recalling memories of a mutual friend and one who stimulated my own interest in the subject as a boy when I read Andrew Green's *Our Haunted Kingdom* (1973). The sadness is in recalling a friend who is no longer with us, at least on an earthly plane, but one who has left us a legacy of his inspiration, ideas and research into numerous haunted sites which Bowen Pearse revisits here.

Every week dozens, perhaps hundreds of people go out on investigations at haunted properties, taking with them a range of equipment from simple thermometers to complex electronic gadgetry. Relatively few realise that the activity in which they are engaging is very much due to the public influence and example of Andrew Green, one of Britain's most active ghost-hunters for some sixty years.

Andrew Green was responsible for the world's first popular book on practical ghost investigation from a scientific perspective, *Ghost Hunting: A Practical Guide* (1973) and widely promoted a rational approach to the whole subject of the paranormal. Earlier researchers and psychic research societies had frequently kept their techniques and findings to themselves or turned investigations into spiritualist séances. In contrast, Andrew Green actively promoted a wholly scientific style of investigation into ghosts and poltergeists. It concentrated on stripping away the folklore, superstition and dogma which all too often surrounded the topic and demonstrated to a wider audience that these mysterious phenomena could be investigated in a rational and scientific manner by anyone with sufficient interest and determination to do so.

Many ghost-hunting techniques such as the use of tape recorders and video equipment championed by Andrew Green in the early 1970s are now standard procedures, but more important than purely technical advice was his emphasis on the mental approach needed for objective investigation. Would-be ghost-hunters need to be rational, open-minded, well balanced in outlook and able to apply common sense, not least to themselves. Ghost hunting should not be about attempting to confirm pre-existing beliefs but trying to learn about a phenomenon which has puzzled humanity for centuries.

Whilst accepting the evidence for psychic phenomena as overwhelming, in Andrew Green rejected the idea that ghosts proved survival after death. Rather than discarnate spirits, he thought the answer to ghost experiences lay in the sub-conscious mind, electromagnetism and the still controversial powers of telepathy and psychokinesis. His views were in keeping with the strong humanist philosophy he maintained throughout his life. His, on occasion frank, remarks in later years ('Borley isn't haunted!' being one) led Andrew Green to be unjustly considered a debunker by some advocates of paranormal. Andrew co-operated with people of goodwill of all faiths and none. Although he would work with mediums he did not uncritically accept the explanations tendered.

One trap that many researchers fall into is one identified by the scientist and ufologist Jacques Vallee. A person may witness a paranormal event, such as an object moving by itself in the presence of a medium. The medium then declares that s/he has moved the object because of the presence of a spirit (or even an alien). In fact there is no independent evidence to support this statement at all. However, having witnessed an inexplicable event the researcher latches on to the first explanation proffered, regardless of actual proof. This is a simple point which many groups and individuals deploying instruments and equipment in search of ghosts could usefully absorb today.

Andrew's willingness to speak and write from a rationalist perspective on ghost hunting led to numerous articles, media appearances and interviews, including debating the existence of ghosts on Radio 4's *You the Jury* and features in a wide range of publications, from *TV Times* to *Police Review* and *Social Work Today*. He was also frequently approached by foreign TV companies seeking an insight into the perceived British obsession with ghosts. Regardless of his own views, Andrew Green always remained respectful and tolerant of differing opinions and admitted he might be wrong. His criticisms were directed against those mediums and super-stitious religious groups who exploited vulnerable people, charlatans who claimed black magic powers and researchers who knowingly passed off fictional ghosts sto-ries as fact. He never ridiculed people who believed themselves spectre stricken.

An understanding of the limits of human perception and the potential for error came in very useful on many occasions. For instance, in 1974 he was able to bring an immediate halt to disturbances in a supposedly haunted house in a Midland city where members of a family had been brought to the brink of suicide in the belief they were being persecuted by an evil spirit.* Peace and sanity were quickly restored to the house by simple reassurance and the application of a little common sense. In the process he discovered the family had been victims of conmen and of sheer nonsense talked by mediums and religious representatives, exacerbating psychological problems rather than reducing them. As a parting shot the alleged ghost was supposed to have rapped, 'I will beat Green!' In characteristic good humour Andrew enquired how the 'ghost' had supposedly spelt Green and how many 'e's it had used. Nothing was heard of it again.

In another case he was able to bring reassurance and a dramatic transformation of the depressive illness of an elderly lady in Hastings who had been told that the spirit of an evil smuggler possessed her home. It was one of a number of occasions when he was thanked by doctors for bringing relief to people plagued by supernatural fears. Unlike some researchers – and this was the one disagreement he had with the approach of the Society for Psychical Research in the past – Andrew Green was not merely prepared to observe suffering and fraud but actually do something about it.

Much of his working in this area, combating the effects of fear and superstition, more resembled social work and counselling rather than psychic research, and has been little publicised. Andrew's work was endorsed by doctors, psychologists and clergymen. In 1982 he was even taken on by Brighton local authority to investigate and report upon allegedly haunted council properties. Indeed, it has been this quality of sensitivity towards the feelings and problems of people apparently suffering from manifestations, which enabled him to successfully solve many cases over the years. It was also what made him a person who is warmly remembered by so many who knew him.

On a personal level, Andrew Green was a great friend and a great example for many of us in the Ghost Club. After admiring his work for many years, I went on to correspond with Andrew and then, via his long-time former Ghost Club chairman Tom Perrott, I was able to meet him and get to know both Andrew and his wife Norah personally. It was a great privilege to get to know Andrew both as a researcher and also to be counted as one of his many friends.

Despite increasing ill-health in the 1990s he continued to broadcast and lecture and in 1996 he held a ghost hunt at the Royal Albert Hall, attended by dozens of journalists. After 1996 failing health prevented him travelling to London but he continued to lecture at Pyke House, Battle in Sussex, where he had begun the world's first part-time evening courses in parapsychology in 1971, on behalf of Hastings College of Further Education. This was a regular feature of the adult education programme for years and despite official retirement in 1998, he continued to participate in a yearly weekend devoted to the paranormal.

The highlight of these weekends was always Andrew's lecture delivered on the Sunday morning before lunch and filled throughout by his gentle humour and sardonic observations. In these he reviewed a selection of his interesting cases, a great number of which have been now been extensively revisited and researched by Bowen Pearse for this book. Such work is long overdue and as well as being a valuable update on many haunted sites, I hope this book will also stimulate interest in Andrew Green's original research and writings.

The writer of a serious ghost book falls between the demands of two audiences. On the one hand there are those who see ghost stories as primarily a superb form of spooky entertainment; on the other are people who are seriously interested in evidence for the paranormal and what it may mean. In this book, I think Bowen Pearse has admirably served the interests of both camps - who frequently overlap in any event.

★(See *Journal of the SPR* Vol. 49 1977-78 pg 41-46)

Introduction

ANDREW GREEN

The man and his work

On a Sunday three months before his death on 21 May 2004, Andrew Green was presented with a cake to celebrate his sixty years as a ghost-hunter. The icing read 'the Spectre Inspector,' a term coined long ago by the *Daily Telegraph* and a title he celebrated as his own. For some six decades, Andrew had roamed the country looking for ghosts, solving people's paranormal problems, reassuring the terrified and collecting spooky material to publish in his many books.

For *Ghost-Hunter's Casebook*, I have gone through hundreds of Andrew's investigations and updated the best. There are even a few so new that Andrew's death prevented him from putting them into print. There are others that Andrew told me about personally but were not published. All these have been included.

Andrew believed in ghosts and defended his position on television, on the radio, in his books and in the many lectures he gave, especially in his always-popular, pioneering adult education classes. In his lifetime, he was a living witness to four ghosts and he himself once became one. After all, he contended, ghosts can include the living.

It really began in September 1944 when a near-fatal experience stimulated a life-long obsession with the paranormal. I first met Andrew in 1967 when we both worked as editors on small magazines put out by the then Thomson Newspapers. One of the first things he told me was of his picture in the *Evening Standard* of the 'suicide tower' and the girl in the window in Ealing – perhaps his most interesting, weird, and unexplained experience.

His father, a senior air-raid warden, was responsible for requisitioning properties in which to store furniture from war-damaged houses. One day he told the seventeen-year-old Andrew that he was visiting a haunted house and would he like to come. The lad jumped at the chance.

Writing later, Andrew remembered it was a glorious autumn day with the sun pouring into the garden. The house was 16 Montpelier Road in Ealing (now demolished) – an address that was to echo down the decades of Andrew's life and appear in many of his articles, talks and books.

Accompanied by his father, the young Andrew began his exploration by climbing to the third floor of the tower roof. When he got to the top, a good 70ft high, he writes that 'slowly a mental image entered my mind to have a look at the garden. Walk over the parapet, it urged. It is only twelve inches onto the lawn. You won't hurt yourself.' But as he began a step down to an almost certain death, his father appeared and grabbed his son by the scruff of the neck and pulled him back. Andrew then knew the explanation as to why twenty other people had lost their lives from this tower. They were recorded as suicides – and he was so very, very close to being suicide number twenty-one.

EARLY YEARS

However, when Andrew Malcolm Green was born on 28 July 1927, in Ealing, London, his family had already experienced paranormal activity. At the birth of one of his brothers twenty-seven years earlier, loud violent crashes were heard as if crockery was being hurled around. It was a family in which Andrew's mother, a semi-professional pianist, and his father, a council executive, lived in separate and opposite sides of the one house. There were rows between his parents whenever they met up and the squabbling was exacerbated at family reunions – by everyone. Andrew didn't think it at all odd that much of his time was taken up nursing his handicapped mother – she suffered from severely ulcerated legs, a result of puerperal fever.

The Greens were an old British family, whose lineage is traceable to before 1400. Over the generations there have been a number of highly placed military men including a general and a vice-admiral. According to Andrew, his mother was an arch snob and as a schoolboy, he was often teased for his 'posh' voice.

Andrew experienced near-death twice in his childhood. At the age of about twelve, he suddenly fell into a coma, which lasted for some ten days. As he was coming round, he heard his father making arrangements for his funeral. A few months later, he was to suffer an out-of-body experience. Sitting in the dentist's chair, he found himself looking down on his own body from the ceiling. He came round with the dentist slapping his face and saying, 'my God, I think he's gone.' Then: 'cancel the ambulance'. Andrew told me that Dr Susan Blackmore, of the Brain Perception Laboratory, University of Bristol, tried to induce out-of-body experiences with drugs and hypnosis and concluded that the incidents were pure imagination. Andrew, however, reached no definite conclusion.

Andrew was aged about thirteen years when an incident occurred that was to be a foretaste of what was to come. He was called to his mother's bedroom where an invisible force was trying to pull the bedclothes off the bed. Andrew tugged against it but such was the strength of the force, he was pulled bodily onto the floor.

Left: *The empty house in Ealing. Photograph taken in 1944 of an empty house in Ealing in which twenty suicides and a number of deaths had occurred. Is the image in the top left-hand window that of Ann Hinchfield who killed herself when only twelve years of age, in 1886?*

Right: *Andrew as a child.*

For economic reasons, Andrew was forced to leave school at fifteen. Feeling he needed to contribute to the family budget, he took on a succession of humdrum jobs. He also joined the Young Conservatives, where he met his first girlfriend (and much later his first wife). He left the Conservative party after writing a controversial article in the *Torch*, a publication put out by the local Ealing Conservative Association. This was his first published article.

He wanted to join the police force but at eighteen, he was too young. In 1945, he was conscripted into the Army and posted into the Life Guards. Andrew was secretary to the colonel and part of his job was to organize visits of VIPs such as the Queen of Holland, Bob Hope and Danny Kaye. During his two years National Service, Andrew performed various ceremonial duties and found himself on duty in Horse Guards Parade on the day of the Queen's wedding on 20 November 1947. He remembered he had 'a first hand grandstand view' of the whole proceedings. But Andrew said that what he remembered best was when he accidentally knocked down the Queen.

ANDREW'S BELIEFS AND WORK

Andrew left the army, aged twenty-one, and sprang back into his role as a ghost-hunter. He founded the Ealing Society for Psychic Phenomena in 1949 – one of several such societies that he set up – becoming its first chairman. With the Ealing society, and alone, he continued to visit haunted houses and conduct experiments in extra-sensory perception. His contact with mediums though, both then and later, persuaded him to have little faith in this branch of the paranormal. This conviction continued throughout his life. He was sure that there was no afterlife in any shape or form – and certainly no spirit to be contacted, to give a message from beyond the grave.

Ghosts were a different story. He fervently believed in them and had his own explanation as to what exactly ghosts are. His ideas were fresh, new and challenging – believed by some, bitterly opposed by others. One theory he loved to propound was that ghosts are formed of 'electromagnetic energy between 380 and 440 "millimicrons" of the infra-red portion of the light spectrum.'

Ghosts as such can be created by people on learning of the sudden and unexpected death of a loved one. Ghosts do not have personalities or intelligence but are a type of electricity situated in a particular locality. They are images of a person or perhaps even a much-loved animal. And – this was something Andrew continually told the afraid – 'Ghosts cannot harm you'.

When, for example, somebody receives a severe and intense shock such as hearing of the death of a spouse or parent, he or she has an immediate image of the dead person where they were last seen. It could be at home, or miles away. It doesn't matter. The image remains at that site and can be seen by any person approaching it whose mind at the time is inactive. This unrelated person unconsciously transfers heat to the area, which recharges the apparition and it becomes visible. This explains, Andrew said, 'why a chill in the air is so often reported by those who see ghosts.' Ghosts by no means have to be a wispy mist. They can appear quite solid with all the colours of their clothes visible, but colours do fade if the spectre remains unseen for a long time.

Andrew also said that surveys reveal that some 70 per cent of witnessed ghosts are of living people – for somebody doesn't have to die to create an image. Many apparitions can be created unconsciously by someone's imagination or strong desire to be in another location. Both smells and sounds can also be recreated at the time of the haunting. They actually become embedded in the building materials and can be regenerated by just the right conditions of moisture and temperature.

DEFENDING GHOSTS ON THE BBC

Two nights before Christmas 1978, BBC Radio 4 broadcast the popular programme, *You the Jury,* with Andrew Green defending the proposition that ghosts exist. As he must have done a thousand times before and since, he defined a ghost. Andrew called it the current idea as to what constitutes a ghost, although perhaps he should have said it was his idea, his definition. Here it is, just as he put it then:

Ghosts exist as an objective form of phenomena, as a type of electricity situated in a particular locality. This static is, we suggest, in a wave pattern, which can be visualized by a person as the transmission from their mind which matches the original impression. The witness feels cold as a result of an electro-chemical process and immediately afterwards sees the ghost.

This cold sensation could well be the catalyst which switches on the mentally recreated picture so to speak. The picture is merely a mental image of some person or a pet animal, the death or injury of which causes intense shock to the creator of that image. This picture is transmitted unconsciously to the actual site and visualised in a telepathic fashion and as such exists.

Andrew's ghosts made him famous. Other writers and researchers like Guy Lyon Playfair – who has written extensively about Britain's haunted world – told me that he has personally never seen a ghost. The same can be said for Tony Cornell, whose recent book, *Investigating the Paranormal*, outlines a lifetime's search; he too told me that he has not had Andrew's experience. Not even one ghost (although it must be said that both men have witnessed poltergeist activity).

But there was also something very special about Andrew. He was born with temporal lobe epilepsy which, according to the British Epilepsy Association, can make one susceptible to paranormal experiences.

ANDREW'S PERSONAL GHOSTS

Andrew met his first ghost in August 1951 in a comfortable B&B in Worthing in Surrey. He settled in for a good night's rest. The next morning, he was woken by a little boy in period dress who had apparently left a welcoming cup of tea by the bedside. Andrew stretched out his arm to take a sip and found the tea cold. He looked round for the boy – he had simply disappeared.

When he went downstairs Andrew told the landlady of his experience. She replied that there was no boy on the premises but that she had left the tea for him the previous night – perhaps he hadn't noticed it. At breakfast, he told his story of the boy to those with whom he shared a table. One of his companions had stayed in Andrew's room before, and he had seen the same boy and heard the same explanation. Apparently, the ghost of the boy from a previous time always appeared to guests in that bedroom. The landlady, afraid that the appearance of a ghost might put people off staying there, always said the same thing – that she had left tea in the room the previous night and it couldn't have been noticed.

Little is known about ghost number two. Andrew was at a neighbour's house when he saw somebody sitting by the window. Andrew said: 'there's a lady you haven't introduced me to.' But as he looked towards her again, 'she simply faded away'. His neighbour listened carefully to Andrew's description. 'That sounds very like my previous wife who died some twelve years ago', he said. Apparently she had been sitting by the same window a few minutes before her death.

This takes us up to ghost number three. In 1971 Andrew was recovering from the unpleasantness of a divorce from his first wife after twenty years of marriage. When the final papers came through, he decided on a modest celebration by himself in Sidmouth in Devon.

He found a good B&B and went to bed early. For no good reason that he knew of then, Andrew woke at precisely 2.15 a.m., shown on his bedside clock, and there in front of him was a brown and white fox terrier. He thought it strange, particularly as there was a house rule forbidding dogs upstairs and anyway, the only dogs in the house downstairs were two cocker spaniels. He watched the fox terrier for perhaps a minute when it simply disappeared. Andrew settled down to sleep again.

The next morning he learned that he was not the only one to see his night visitor. Six others had also seen the fox terrier in that room over the past year. But the explanation was brutal. The previous house owners had had a fox terrier named Spot; he had strayed onto the road and been squashed by a passing car. Significantly, the time had been 2.15 a.m. in the morning. Andrew now understood what had awoken him at this time.

In Andrew's 1977 *Phantom Ladies,* he refers briefly to the fourth ghost. It was an evening in 1971, near Buxted, in East Sussex. He was heading for home along Tuck's Lane. Andrew didn't know it then but the lane had a sad history: in the seventeenth century, a Nan Tuck was persecuted and driven from the village, the crowd yelling that she was a witch. She ran away down the lane which now bears her name but the ordeal had been too much for her. The following day, her dead body was found hanging from a tree. Apparently, she was devoutly buried.

Leaving Buxted on his way home, Andrew drove down Nan's Lane. He was puzzled by a shadow which persistently kept just in front of his headlights moving in the hedgerow. Risking blocking the twisty road, he stopped to check his headlights. He said, 'there was no cause for the peculiar impression so I resumed my journey, but for at least half a mile this human-sized and human-shaped darkness kept flitting along. Then suddenly it was not there any more.'

Some two months later, he learned the story of Nan Tuck for the first time.

ANDREW THE GHOST

Those were the ghosts Andrew experienced in a lifetime but there was a fifth spectre – and this ghost was Andrew himself.

This story really begins in his Guildford garden, shortly before his 1971 divorce. He had become obsessed with the potential of his one-acre garden and had decided to make a large rockery. Every spare minute went into its creation and he wonders now if paying more attention to his rockery rather than to his wife might well have hastened the divorce. Hazel never liked gardening.

A cartoon of Andrew by Fred Towers.

After Hazel left him, Andrew sold the house to an engineer and his family from Harrow. They had a twelve-year-old daughter whom Andrew had never met. Some months later, the engineer and his family came round to visit Andrew in his new house at Iden. They were not prepared for what happened next. Nobody was. As they gathered around the door, the daughter stood at the back and had not yet seen Andrew. But as it turned out, she had seen him – many times. More often than she realized. More often than she would have liked.

After her parents had made their introductions, it was her turn and she came forward. One look at Andrew and she fainted. Clean out. Andrew was much puzzled. 'I've seen you before many times Mr Green', she said on recovering. 'On the rockery in the garden – your rockery that you sold to us.' It was Andrew's ghost she had seen – a live ghost. And she had not been ready to greet him in the flesh.

She fainted a second time and when she came round, she pinched Andrew's arm to make sure that 'this one' this time was real. Andrew's comment was that the incident confirmed his theory that a mental image of a ghost can be created by someone's strong desire to be in another location. He dearly missed working in his rockery.

THE GHOST-HUNTER AS COUNSELLOR

In 1961, aged thirty-four, Andrew became the co-founder of the Institute of Service Management. He was later group editor with the Trade and Technical Press. Throughout his lifetime, Andrew had a variety of jobs – industrial chemist, PR man and magazine editor. He took a science degree and an M.Phil at the London School of Economics. He even set up his own publishing firm.

But ghost-hunting remained his greatest passion. In 1956 he investigated the well known 'poltergeist girl of Battersea.' The girl claimed that she was haunted by the spirit of Donald Capet, a dead member of the French monarchy. Andrew received a letter from the spirit – although he knew full well it was written by the girl herself. This got into the *Guinness Book of Records* as the only known letter written by a poltergeist. Somehow Andrew felt proud to have the entry, despite the extenuating circumstances. It was apparently one of many such letters sent out.

But poltergeist activity is only one of many varied instances in Andrew's *Our Haunted Kingdom* and one of many problems a ghost-hunter is expected to tackle. He needs to be a doctor, a counsellor, a psychiatrist, even a marriage-broker and a detective, often all at the same time. Around the time of the publication of Andrew's bestseller, there were several interesting cases all to do with council properties. At the time, they could not be published for reasons of confidentiality, but the years have gone by and they are reported here for the first time.

There was the case of the Haunted Marriage Bed – related in the body of this book – when Andrew became a marriage counsellor.

In the next case, the researcher dons the mantle of a general practitioner. A couple, whom we shall call Barbara and Alex, had recently moved into a local council house where Barbara had been plagued by an unseen voice, apparently that of the previous owner, recently dead, whom Barbara heard loudly calling out, 'this is my house. Get out! Get out!' The tenant mentioned this to the council who, convinced of the serious nature of the repeated incidents, called for the services of a 'ghost-hunter'. A councillor had previously been to one of Andrew's adult lectures and he asked Andrew if he would assist.

Andrew agreed and he followed his usual procedure and asked for the name of the couple's GP with permission to contact him if he felt it was necessary. The doctor admitted that Barbara had been on the same strong medication for depression for some time but had not been back to the surgery to check the treatment. It turned out that the patient had been afraid to go for another consultation as she suspected she might be sent to a psychiatrist – a course of action the doctor admitted would have probably taken place. The medication was immediately cancelled and replaced with another more suitable. The result was that the client no longer heard the mysterious, horrifying voices or suffered the irrational fear and is no longer 'under the doctor'.

In another case, in the Midlands, the wife, whom we shall call Helen, was suffering horrific hallucinations, to the point where the whole family were considering suicide.

They had contacted the police, two or three religious groups and unfortunately a couple of self-styled 'spirit healers', one of whom charged them an outrageous £100 on each weekly visit to ensure their home was 'ghost free'.

After meeting the family and observing their actions for several hours, Andrew realised that he found it was another case calling for contact with their doctor. The medication Helen was taking had precise instructions on the bottle – but these were being ignored. The tablets were to be taken early and Helen took them late. There was a warning that anybody taking the drug should never eat cheese during the course of treatment but Helen loved her cheese sandwiches just before going to bed with the pills. And as if this wasn't enough to be causing hallucinations and hysteria, the family lived next to a cemetery where vandals would often leave the corpse of a dog or cat on a tombstone – 'just for fun.' As a rationalist Andrew has experienced many such cases when the solution appears to be fairly simple. It was the same with this case. As soon as the family carried out the instructions on the new medicine's label and followed everything their GP had to say, all was well.

THE REASON WHY

Why did Andrew do it? Why did he travel all over the country only to advise that somebody should change their medication? In such cases, Andrew asked for no money except his travelling expenses. He does it, he told me, because of the great satisfaction he feels. Andrew was rather like that. A quiet, polite man with a strong professional streak, who insisted that everything must be honest and above board. He would say: 'I am simply trying to rationalise and offset the scare mongering and hysteria-provoking material proffered by some fanatics, often supported by undesirable aspects of the media.'

He sadly divorced his first wife in 1971 but made an important step in his career. He introduced the first twenty-five-week course evening classes on the paranormal. This proved so popular that he gave courses in Surrey, Kent, Sussex, Cambridge and London. Once established, they continued after Andrew left. In 1972, he became a member of the Society for Psychical Research and remained a member until his death in 2004.

By 1971, he had gathered so much ghostly material that he decided to put it all in one book. *Our Haunted Kingdom* was the result and with publication in hardback and then paperback, the book proved a minor bestseller.

This was followed by *Ghost-Hunting, a Practical Guide*, the world's first book devoted to scientific ghost hunting techniques and still the best book on the subject. He promoted the use of tape-recorders, film and thermometers in investigations - all of which have become standard equipment among ghost-hunters. Andrew emphasised that the explanations for many ghostly phenomena lay within the human mind, involving as-yet-unexplained powers of telepathy and psycho kinesis. The book ran to several editions and was translated into Italian.

PERFECT MARRIAGE AT LAST

In 1973, Andrew was called to investigate a house in which perfume at times wafted in the air and no one knew why. He was able to explain that the perfume had seeped into the timber of the cottage and was released whenever a fire was lit.

But this also turned out to be perhaps the most significant investigation of his life. For the owner of the perfumed house would in time become his second wife – the teacher and poet, Norah Cawthorne. Norah had frankly wondered what the fuss was all about, despite the fact that two students boarding with her had fled in fright. Why had they left so rapidly?

It was for more than one incident and several things added together. Norah's tenants had heard unexplained footsteps in the middle of the night. That was the beginning. And one of the students, a girl, woke to find a tall man in a blue dressing gown at the foot of her bed. She screamed and he went away: 'just disappeared', she said. Later, the same figure was seen coming down the stairs heading for the bathroom. Norah wasn't at all frightened. Yes, she remembered, Daddy did have a blue dressing gown. She somehow thought it was all quite natural. Many years later, in the days after she lost Andrew, she told me that she had waited in vain for a signal from the grave. Just a whisper, a signal, some form of contact.

Left: *Andrew and Norah on their wedding day.*

Right: *Sixty years a ghost-hunter. Celebratory cake presented to Andrew by Alan Murdie, legal advisor to the Ghost Club.*

Norah loved the perfume and called it 'wonderful.' And out of all this came friendship, love and then marriage in 1979. The couple enjoyed twenty-five years of happy married life together.

At first Norah had found all this talk of ghosts something of a brave new world. But her students leaving was affecting her income, so she had to take it seriously. But what were her first thoughts about Andrew? She had the impression he looked rather ill. She thought he need feeding and looking after.

She remembered that soon after meeting Andrew, she went on a 'wee' holiday with an actress friend (Norah had been a student at RADA). 'What does he do?' her friend asked. 'He's a parapsychologist', Norah answered. 'And what the hell is that?' Norah struggled with an explanation: 'It's a scientific study of the unscientific.' The two friends collapsed into peals of laughter.

But closer contact with Andrew changed her mind completely. It was definitely no laughing matter. Norah saw how sensitively he handled other people's problems and put their often fractured lives together. She also came to learn there were a lot of charlatans in Andrew's profession – some charging £100 a day (then a tidy sum). Andrew, on the other hand, charged nothing except expenses. Norah was drawn to him, she says. But both were 'romantically entangled' with somebody else. Norah was nevertheless a free woman – her husband had left her for somebody else back in 1966 and she had obtained a divorce in 1967. Real romance – and marriage to Andrew – would come later.

In the meantime, she liked the way Andrew explained things – very down-to-earth and sensible. She accepted what had been seen – it was her father and he had come for a visit. That was that. Andrew identified the smell as coming from the mimosa plant. And eventually, all the haunting simply 'dissolved in time'. Her father must have been 'fed up', she reckons – 'so he simply went away'.

TWILIGHT YEARS – ANDREW'S TERM

In his last years – Andrew was much weakened by the emphysema that eventually killed him – Andrew continued to collect ghosts and put them into book form. Book followed book and by the time of his death, sixteen had been published – the seventeenth posthumously. He would still respond to an approach by someone believing they were being haunted (insisting he was given the name of the GP first in case the experiences were related to that person's physical or mental health), and still gave the occasional lecture. He was still writing almost up to the day of his death.

Andrew died on 21 May 2004, aged seventy-six.

BOWEN PEARSE
KENT, SEPTEMBER 2007

ONE

Bedfordshire

CHICKSANDS PRIORY

A walled-up nun and other free spirits

To see this fine and ancient building on a bright summer's morning, it is hard to imagine the blood-stained goings-on that have taken place within its walls and the ghosts that have walked its corridors.

The history of Chicksands Priory goes back a long way. The priory was founded by Payne de Beauchamp and his wife, the Countess Rohese, between 1147 and 1153. The countess's first husband was Geoffrey de Maudeville, first Earl of Essex and founder of Walden Abbey.

After Geoffrey's death in 1144 and his widow's remarriage, she turned her attention to Cudessand, the original name for the area in the eleventh century. The priory was well endowed, being the third largest religious house of the Gilbertine order in England. It was one of the nine two-cloistered establishments that accommodated canons, nuns, lay brothers and lay sisters. At one time, it may well have housed over 200 people.

In March 1536 the suppression of small monasteries under Henry VIII began. Two years later, in October 1538, accepting their fate, all in the priory surrendered the building. These included John Orrey, sub-prior of Chicksands, six canons and seventeen nuns and Margaret Burton, the prioress. They were all pensioned off.

New owners followed in quick succession – Richard Snowe in 1540, Sir Peter Osborne in 1587 and his descendents until Sir Algernon Osborn (seventh baronet), who died in 1948, having sold the estate to the Crown in 1936. Three years later, at the beginning of the Second World War, the Crown Commissioners gave the use of Chicksands to the Royal Navy and after a lapse of only nine months the RAF took over the tenancy. In November 1950 they were joined by the United States Air Force personnel who remained there until 1955.

There are numerous legends about the priory, the most well known being that of the disgraced nun whose affair with a canon resulted in the girl's pregnancy. The punishment was death – a quick end for the man, less so for the nun. She was partially walled up to her neck, enabling her to witness the execution of her lover. She was then completely

Chicksands Priory was founded in the twelfth century. (Courtesy of the Friends of Chicksands Priory)

walled up and allowed to die. It is said that on the seventeenth of every month, the ghost of the nun walks about the priory searching in vain for her lost lover.

The nun is commemorated on a plaque over one of the windows in the eastern wall of the remaining cloister and is named as Rosata: 'By virtues guarded and by manners graced, here alas is the fair Rosata placed.' Experts, however, claim that the plaque is an eighteenth-century invention. No medieval use of this Christian name has been found.

Quite aside from Rosata, there is evidence of further goings-on at what should have been a place of total abstinence. In 1535, Dr Richard Layton wrote to Thomas Cromwell saying that on visiting the priory he discovered 'two of the said nuunnes [sic] not baron,' one of them having been impregnated by a serving man, the other by a superior.

There are numerous accounts of long-ago walled-up nuns left to die but recent research carried out by author Alan Murdie puts the kibosh on the whole idea. During the medieval period nuns were occasionally walled up but apparently at their own request. It was a matter of total retreat and extreme religious zeal. But once walled up, her head was free so she could be fed and watered. (I must ask Alan how they managed with the loo.)

There are also stories of these nuns becoming ghosts though the evidence is very sketchy. But there have been other ghosts at Chicksands, right up to the present day. There is even a story of a man scared to death by the appearance of a ghost – but no details have been found. In the 1960s, a figure of a woman dressed in black was seen disappearing through a wall in the picture gallery adjoining King James's room. The apparition had long hair covering most of its features – not exactly the appearance of a nun.

Back in January 1915, one of the female staff said she saw a 'fascinating woman dressed in white glide past me. I heard the rustle of her dress and saw the long white train as she moved past.' The time was around 10 p.m.

In August 1954, a spine-tingling apparition appeared before a flight lieutenant. On coming off duty at ten at night, he went to his room to read but fell asleep. He awoke at around 3.45 a.m. and again decided to read for a while and switched on the light. He recalled with horror what he saw – 'there at the side of my bed was a woman with a ruddy face and untidy hair wearing a dark dress with a white lace collar. She appeared to be holding a notepad. She moved to the foot of my bed and vanished.'

Three years later, in March 1957, another officer recalled what he had seen in the picture-gallery. 'It was a motionless head and shoulders of a middle-aged woman dressed in what we associate as a nun's head-dress. She was looking past me with an expression of serious thought.' In another experience, an American officer said he had felt an amorphous pair of hands wrapped around his ankles.

The priory itself was magnificently restored by the Ministry of Defence in 1997-98. It is open to the public strictly by appointment, on the first and third Sunday afternoons of the month, April to October. The number to ring is 01525 860497.

CHICKSANDS PRIORY
SHEFFORD, BEDFORDSHIRE
ENTRY STRICTLY BY APPOINTMENT, SEE ABOVE

WOBURN ABBEY

The stately ghosts of Woburn

Woburn Abbey, the magnificent home of the Dukes of Bedford for some 400 years, houses one of the world's most important art collections. The abbey also provides a refuge for ghost after ghost, continuing up to the present day. The latest apparition, appearing over the last couple of years, managed to frighten three visitors in the public area of the vaults. According to the duke, the ghost simply 'appeared and disappeared before them'. The very presence of ghosts certainly makes Woburn more interesting, but the staff are also eager not to put people off coming. So the report to me, following the latest sighting, contained this reassurance: none of the three visitors found the appearance of an apparition materialising and dematerialising in front of them 'at all upsetting'.

But the bloody hand of history has also left its mark. One of the more recent hauntings concerned a very unfortunate black manservant, to the third Duke of Bedford. Burglars broke into the mansion in a a daylight raid. They found the servant, whom we shall call Charlie, and beat him, threatening to continue the violence until he showed them the whereabouts of more treasure. He loyally refused to tell them a thing, so they strung him up to the point of near strangulation. Still refusing to talk, they then locked him in a cupboard in the Masquerade Room while they plundered the house and collected their loot.

The poor servant was by now in a pretty poor state but they had not finished with him yet. They first threw him out of the window, which nearly killed him. They then made sure of his death by throwing the poor bloke into the lake and drowning him. His ghost, whose actions began in the 1960s – has been known to open and close doors, just as a good servant should. Witnesses have claimed that he opens a door at one end of the room as if someone were walking in. The ghost allows that person time to cross the room until – you hear the footsteps – he opens the door at the other side.

To everyone's chagrin, Charlie's spirit tried this in the television room. It was similar to the above. According to the duke, 'we'd be sitting there when suddenly the handle of the door at one end of the room would turn and the door would open just as though an invisible person was coming through.' Steps were taken to stop the ghost's behaviour. The doors were constantly locked and unlocked. Finally, fed up with the draughts – in an act of desperation – the locks were changed. (You might as well try to stop a cyclone with a broad sword.) Charlie's actions continued.

The duke suggested a structural alteration might just solve the problems. Rooms were remodelled so that Charlie's haunting ground became a corridor. But Charlie has continued to haunt other parts of the mansion. The duke and duchess would be sitting comfortably in another room when they suffered an 'uncomfortable' feeling. They wouldn't put it stronger than that. Then, as if it had just come from the lake, a watery hand touched their faces.

But the door openings and closings didn't stop with the television room. Andrew writes that in conversation with Her Grace, the previous Duchess of Bedford, she explained how house guests became perturbed when their (three) bedroom doors opened of their own accord. They had had to get out of bed several times during the night to close them. They were apparently unaware of Woburn's ghosts and their little tricks. (Had nobody told them what to expect?)

The abbey hasn't always been a happy place. In their private apartments, the duke and duchess have found a restless, uncomfortable atmosphere that they find hard to describe. Tom Corbett, a clairvoyant, once visited the abbey and he found the top floor rooms in particular, 'soaked in unhappiness over many lifetimes, leaving an overpowering atmosphere of misery, strong enough to affect people.' There is a 'malaise' about the Wood Library and the duke's office.

The duke also felt the presence of his late grandmother, 'The Flying Duchess', in the isolated little summer house on the west side of the park and flitting around the gardens. This is the phantom of Lady Mary Tribe, who married the eleventh duke and so came to live at Woburn.

Lady Mary was an adventurous woman who, in the 1920s, became involved in the then glamorous business of flying. She was the first woman to fly to South Africa, visiting many British colonial settlements on the way. She made great efforts to encourage other women to take up flying, both as a career move and in sport. She lost her life in 1937, flying off the coast of East Anglia. Her gentle spirit entered the grounds of Woburn soon afterwards.

The first stirrings of the Woburn story must begin sometime before AD 969 when there was a Saxon hamlet by that name, the word's derivation being 'w', meaning crooked, and 'burn', a small stream. But the most significant date is probably 1145, when Cistercian monks from Fountains Abbey in Yorkshire under Hugh de Bolebec founded an abbey at Woburn.

In 1538, on the Dissolution of the Monasteries, the abbot of Woburn, Robert Hobbes, was executed for treason, after speaking out about Henry VIII's annulment of his first marriage and remarriage to Anne Boleyn. The story, carried over the centuries, was that the abbot and two of his clerics were executed and left hanging from the branch of an oak tree near the south front of the house. And beneath where their bodies once dangled, not a blade of grass nor a flower will grow. Along with so many others across the country, the abbey was dissolved in 1538.

The present mansion was begun on the site in 1744 by the fourth Duke of Bedford and it is this man, John Russell, who filled the house with the amazing art collection that people queue to see today.

With this background, it is not surprising that some of the ghosts at Woburn are monks. During a function in the fabulous Sculpture Room in March 1971, guests saw a figure in a brown habit by the entrance pillars which rapidly disappeared through a doorway. The monks must have been a lecherous lot, for all their holy habits, as women have complained of being groped by invisible hands.

An identical ghost dressed in a monk's habit was seen in the crypt, believed to be the ghost of Robert Hobbes, the abbot who was hanged due to his opposition to Henry VIII's marriage to Anne Boleyn. The thirteenth duke, John, says that the phantom was dressed in pale grey. If brown, it couldn't be the abbot – as claimed – since Cistercian monks wear white. Lay brothers wore brown but with a black garment over it. The crypt is out of bounds to the general public.

Thus are the ghosts of Woburn Abbey, yesterday, today, and tomorrow – who knows, they keep coming. Take a good look round when you come to visit. You never know what/whom you may find.

WOBURN ABBEY

WOBURN, BEDFORDSHIRE,

TEL: 01525 290666.

OPEN AT THE APPROPRIATE HOURS.

TWO

Berkshire

LITTLECOTE HOUSE

Wild Will's hideous murder

Littlecote House, a beautiful Tudor mansion dating from around 1490 and now a hotel, boasts a number of ghosts, ancient and modern. The earliest of these date from Elizabethan times and owe their grisly origins mainly to the behaviour of 'Wild Will', the black sheep of the wealthy Darrell family, who then owned the mansion.

Imagine the pain, the joy and the great risk of death surrounding a birth in fifteenth century England. See the mother exhausted and happy with her new-born, the midwife hot and sweaty from her hard work and carrying the infant securely in her arms. Then see Wild Will appear, angry and cruel. He speaks to the midwife, determined that his orders be carried out. 'Throw the little bastard onto the fire,' he barks. She hesitates, refuses, pleads, holds the wee baby more tightly. But Will will not be defied. He tears the baby from the midwife's arms. He tosses the small bundle onto the centre of the fire in the grate, holding it down with his well polished boot until the infant had been consumed by the flames.

Somehow, Will is acquitted of the murder, probably through family connections. But nobody is sure who the baby was. There are several theories. But most are sure that the child was Will's – born to one of his several mistresses, possibly even his own sister.

Since then – from time to time up to the present day – the ghost of the tragic, unidentified, fair-haired mother has been seen, carrying a light. Someone witnessed the apparition of the midwife – Mrs Barnes of Sheffield – carrying the baby in her arms. Whoever the ghost was, it took its revenge. Shortly after the murder, they say the ghost of the child is supposed to have appeared to Wild Will when he was out riding in the park. The horse shied to such an extent that Will was thrown from the saddle and broke his neck. The exact spot where he died, Darrell's Stile, still frightens horses.

But Will's death in no way ended the story. The ghost still haunts the room where the child was roasted alive. There have been a number of sightings. In 1927 the apparition of the mother was seen by Sir Edward Wills, elder brother of previous

Visit Littlecote House for a very ghostly few days.

owners, the Wills, the wealthy tobacco family; and again, more recently, by the staff of the new owners, Bourne Leisure/Warner Breaks.

But other modern ghosts still lie in wait for the unwary, not all reported in Andrew's time. In updating this entry, I spoke to Deborah Wood, the hotel's marketing manager; she told me a strange story, related to her by a guest who came there on holiday in 2005. This guest, whom we shall call Anne, had heard the story from her great aunt about the ghostly red bloodstains on the wooden floor in front of the fireplace in the haunted bedroom. Apparently, the bloodstains appeared during the winter and nothing but nothing could remove them. Something more drastic was called for. Anne's grandfather, a carpenter, was summoned to replace the wooden flooring on which the stains appeared. Drastic though it was, it seemed to be the only way the house could be rid of the bloodstains and their ghastly associations.

In recent times, first a journalist, then several television crews, have come looking for ghosts. (But, as Andrew said to me many times, no ghost will ever appear if you lie in wait for it). A Meridian Television crew paid a visit at Halloween, 2003 – loaded up with a lot of electrical ghost-testing apparatus. The crew bravely set up their equipment in the haunted bedroom and settled down to wait for something to happen, something to capture on film. But according to Deborah, they ran away in the early hours of the following morning. The lone journalist who had come on an earlier date did the same. It seems that this has now become almost standard behaviour for anyone trying to sleep in the haunted bedroom – running scared late at night.

There are now nine new luxury suites in the old manor house, and one of these has a ghostly story to tell. A guest left his room with all his things tidily put away in the cupboard and then went down to dinner. He returned to his suite to find his tidily arranged belongings scattered to the four winds – common evidence of poltergeist activity. No other poltergeist experiences were reported to me.

Andrew once said that children were the most susceptible to paranormal behaviour and Deborah had a story about youngsters in the hotel. Littlecote House has for some time employed house-guides who do everything to make guests happy. In 1993 a guide brought a party of children to the chapel; one little boy called out in fright: 'what's that arm doing there?' The guide looked in the direction where the lad was pointing – and there, sure enough, for all to see, was an unattached arm with a hand on the end of it, walking along the tops of the pews. Two weeks later, the guide saw the same arm again. Nobody had any explanation.

Another paranormal arm appeared in 2004. A Holistic Fair was to be held in the orangery. One member of the organizing committee came for an initial inspection. She reported that the same unattached arm gripped her arm tight and continued the grip until she was outside the front of the house. But the simple ghost of an unattached arm wasn't enough to stop the Fair. Perhaps it made the booking more exciting!

Past owners of the mansion, the Wills family, also employed guides to look after their guests. They left this story. The guides reported that when anyone stood in front of the fire with their hands behind them, the backs of their hands were gently brushed 'as by a child'. Other people, susceptible to such things, reported that they felt that the house was filled with children – although no children were present at the time.

Back in the 1970s Andrew reported that in 1968, the apparition of a female figure had been seen walking along one of the narrow passages in the house, through a doorway on the north side and out into the garden. In 1969, when all the guests had left the house, the hotel staff heard mysterious, unknown footsteps in the Long Gallery.

A year later, Joe Milburn, a National Trust lecturer, took two photographs of the four-poster bed in the haunted bedroom. When the film was developed an unusual semi-transparent shape could be seen leaning though the curtains surrounding the bed. Kodak assured Joe that there was nothing wrong with the film: their technicians had checked it and found it perfect. They did, however, report that film can show what the eye cannot see.

Andrew would be pleased to hear – from the other side of the grave – that the Littlecote ghosts he first reported are still in full cry.

LITTLECOTE HOUSE
NEAR HUNGERFORD, BERKSHIRE
OPEN TO THE PUBLIC AS A SHORT-BREAK HOTEL
TEL: 01488 682509

THREE

Buckinghamshire

CHURCH OF ST PETER AND ST PAUL

The ghost who would be organist

It's happening now. Church organist Tom Clark is convinced that a being from another world is constantly interfering with the pedals and stops of his old Victorian organ. Was it perhaps wanting an organ for itself? If a ghost is behaving this way lately, it would by no means be the first time. As Andrew pens in his original entry, there were similar goings-on shortly after the Second World War. A ghost was seen to open the front door of the church and 'just glide towards one of the memorial tablets where it vanished'.

St Peter and St Paul, Ellesborough. Ghosts have been seen in the church.

Church of St Peter and St Paul. (courtesy of Dr Ralph Wynroe)

Then there was the experience of two ladies of the parish. It was a summer evening with sunlight slanting through the windows while the ladies sat arranging flowers. One of them walked to the back of the church where she saw two women in old fashioned clothes – perhaps from the 1920s or 1930s – seated on a pew. But then, moments later, they 'simply disappeared by gliding through the thick walls of the church.'

And that's by no means all. A local publication, *The Church on the Hill*, by Gerald W. Line, describes 'a ghostly visitor in seventeenth century dress that could be the spirit of a former rector, the Revd Robert Wallis.' The rector held the post twice – from 1635 to 1637 and again from 1665 to 1667. Perhaps he felt he just could not leave the old church he loved so much. The book also refers to another possible ghostly candidate for the church's resident – poor Thomas Emery who died of the plague.

Whoever it might be, the present church warden, Enid Alford, is convinced that ghosts exist – but is uncertain whether they are actually in her church. Somehow, I don't think that Tom Clark would agree with her. Ghosts have a habit of not doing what you expect.

CHURCH OF ST PETER AND ST PAUL,
ELLESBOROUGH, BUCKINGHAMSHIRE
OPEN TO THE PUBLIC

GEORGE & DRAGON HOTEL

The very profitable ghosts

The television cameras roll, special Haunting Breaks are organised and anxious guests book up ahead hoping to be put into the spooky room 10 where it's all happened and where the haunting is. And the cause of this clamour is the fact that this delightful hotel is – whisper it – haunted. The proprietor, Susan Raines, told me she doesn't quite believe in ghosts. Not yet. Though some say she's gradually losing the battle: ghosts are colonising her hotel.

Susan actually would have good reason to believe in the odd spectre. She has experienced some very ghostly goings-on. Here are some of the spooky things that have happened to her: while she was decorating, the taps in the nearby bathroom came on all at once – and there was nobody there; various unattended vacuum cleaners started up; paint brushes took flight from one side of the room to another; she saw a young lad carrying on a lively conversation with someone in an armchair whom nobody else could see. And there are a lot more strange happenings to keep the television companies interested and Susan scared.

Buckinghamshire

Back in the early 1970s when Andrew was writing his *Our Haunted Kingdom*, he pointed out that the hotel is situated not far from the notorious Hell Fire Caves, the site of Francis Dashwood's diabolical orgies in the eighteenth century. The then owner of the hotel, a Mr Jones, seemed to be in the minority of those who had not seen the ghost which went by the name of Susie (or Sukie). He had not witnessed her activities, nor for that matter had he heard ghostly footsteps treading the main staircase.

In January 1972, one of the hotel guests saw the apparition of a young woman in a 'glorious white dress' gliding along an upstairs passage. Mr Jones also said that dogs refused to enter the bedroom where the ghost had been seen.

But who was the ghost and where did it originate? One theory was that the ghost was that of an attractive serving wench dressed all in white who was accidentally killed in the nearby caves by three jealous admirers some 250 years ago. The girl had been strongly attracted to one of the more generous and prosperous local men and no doubt she had been lured to the assignation in the belief she was meeting her lover. One can imagine the horror with which she viewed a trio of half-drunk sneering men and must have fought fiercely before tripping and hitting her head on the cave wall (if that is to be believed). The next day her body was discovered and brought back to what is now called the haunted bedroom, still dressed in what could almost be mistaken for a wedding dress.

There was a report in a 1966 *Readers Digest* by an American guest who had slept in the haunted bedroom. He was abruptly roused from his sleep by a 'column of light hovering near the doorway. The light ballooned forward and seemed to reach towards me.' He was already out of bed, armed with – what was nearest to hand – a heavy book. But when the swishing opaqueness moved towards him, he jumped back and turned on the light. The apparition had gone.

But what about the heavy footsteps on the stairs? They say that this was the tread of a traveller who, it was claimed, was robbed, murdered and locked away in another room (the haunted room perhaps?) in the latter half of the eighteenth century.

Mr James, the then proprietor, also told Andrew that there was talk of an existing but partly buried underground tunnel linking the hotel with the Hell Fire Caves. Such a link may perhaps be thought very appropriate.

GEORGE & DRAGON HOTEL
HIGH STREET, WEST WYCOMBE, BUCKINGHAMSHIRE
TEL: 01494 464414
EMAIL: ENQ@GEORGE-AND-DRAGON.CO.UK
OPEN AT THE APPROPRIATE HOURS

FOUR

Cambridgeshire

HINCHINBROOKE SCHOOL

Unexplained noises remain the most common occurrence

Back in the 1970s when Andrew Green was compiling his highly successful *Ghosts of Today*, Hinchinbrooke School's curator, Rodney Stratford, told him about the school building's ancient origins that went some way towards explaining today's hauntings. During the Middle Ages, this was a nunnery (a community of either sex in those days). The curator told of many instances of a ghost of a monk being seen, as well as a phantom dog. Another witness was apparently the ninth Earl of Sandwich.

The present-day witness to those 'unexplained noises' is the school's heritage advisor, Mr T.R. Wheeler. According to Mr Wheeler, there have been recent sightings of nuns both in the house and about the grounds. At times with no children about, there have been sounds of children playing, voices whispering, and unknown footsteps. Mr Wheeler told me that – for some unknown reason – such activity is more likely to occur during building work.

During the Second World War, the building was requisitioned and used as a Red Cross Hospital. It was during this time that a Mr B. Ward, previously of Richmond, also saw the ghost of a nun in the nurses' dormitory. Most certainly 'unexplained'.

HINCHINBROOKE SCHOOL
NUNNERY COURT, HUNTINGDON, CAMBRIDGESHIRE

FIVE

Cornwall

—◆————◆—

CHAPEL STREET

A mean she-devil of a ghost

Back in the early 1800s a mansion stood in Chapel Street, Penzance, and behind it was a large orchard with the most succulent fruit. The apples, ripe, rosy and sweet, were specially prized. The owner of the big mansion and the prize orchard was a Mrs Baines, and you would not find such a scrooge-like harridan anywhere in Cornwall. No thieving children, no 'scrumpers' were going to get a taste of her beautiful fruit. She'd rather those rosy beauties would fall and rot on the ground.

Mrs Baines posted a twenty-four-hour armed guard on the orchard. She could move about during the day, sneaking around, spying, making sure no one on her payroll (on starvation wages) was not fully on duty and daring to pick any fruit for themselves. It might have been a diamond mine she owned.

But night was a problem for Mrs Baines. She had to sleep sometime. So how could she always supervise what was going on? She held no one on trust. So one dark, moonless night she sneaked around herself seeing if her night-duty man, John, (according to Andrew's *Ghosts of Today*, an old fisherman) was fully awake, and keeping his blunderbuss ready cocked. She looked, she peered, she crept around, but no John.

John was there all right, taking forty winks behind a hedge. Mrs Baines decided to be a pretend thief, so gave one of the apple trees a good shaking – to give the perfect pretence that she herself was a fruit thief. Swish, swish, swish-tumble. The sound was enough to waken John (he was a light sleeper). He moved quickly, got to his feet and saw the dark outline of the thief, barely discernable in the black night. Now he was alert, John brought up the blunderbuss to his shoulder and hit the hiding Mrs Baines amidships.

Well, the lady soon shrugged off her mortal coil and became the best watch-woman the orchard ever had. Her ghost could be seen, flitting through the foliage, counting the number of fruit on each tree just in case it had changed from last time.

Now she could do what mortals couldn't: she herself could carry out a twenty-four-hour guard. With time, the beautiful rosy fruit would ripen and then fall. She didn't mind. And with her powdered hair, lace cap, ruffles, and silk mantle, and carrying her gold-headed cane, she was easily recognised by all who had known her in life.

Her ghost was seen underneath the tree where she was shot, or walking around the orchard. Periodically she was seen at the top of the wall, and, to perch on top for a moment before vanishing. But just frightening people who dared to come near her orchid was not enough. She began to haunt the house as well, adopting the antics of poltergeist. She would slam doors, rattle furniture, and get amongst the glass and crockery.

The time had come — as it does to many — to try and see what a man of God could do. The parson tried, mumbled all he was supposed to mumble, and practised his ritual acts. But all this had only partial success with our ghost. She was not so obtrusive as she had been, but she has been seen near the top end of Chapel Street where she has been doing one of those things ghosts do best — disappearing through the wall. Any wall. Often.

CHAPEL STREET
PENZANCE, CORNWALL
OPEN ALL HOURS

An early engraving of Chapel Street. A ghost is not far away. (courtesy of the Cornish Studies Library)

Hell's Mouth is in the foreground, Deadman's Cove in the near middle distance. The precipitous cliffs meant death for the smuggler. (courtesy of the Cornish Studies Library)

HELLS MOUTH AND DEADMAN'S COVE

The last scream

The smugglers in Cornwall in the eighteenth century asked for no quarter and gave none. They knew that if caught they would be hanged – and they may have known the old proverb 'you might as well be hanged for a sheep as a lamb', so they never balked at murder, torture, and mayhem.

The cliffs of Hell's Mouth, on the north coast of Cornwall, and a short distance from Dead Man's Cove, are high and dangerous. Below them is a network of tunnels and underground caves stretching for a great distance. For hundreds of years these caves had been used by smugglers to store brandy, tobacco, and other highly desirable items. The government's high taxation on these goodies, to pay for the Napoleonic Wars, only encouraged the trade, for there was a great deal of crooked money to be made.

But the Cornish smugglers who operated around Deadman's Cove in the eighteenth century were a particularly brutish and violent gang who would kill without compunction. They had strong proprietorial feelings about their loot and would guard it with their lives.

Two of the most bloodthirsty members of the gang were brothers, who seemed to match each other in degrees of ruthlessness and barbarism. Finally, after years of trying to track them down, the authorities caught up with them. The younger of the two brothers met the usual slow death by hanging, in front of a large, jeering crowd.

But the remaining brother somehow avoided capture and continued his life of crime, only now with increased vigour. It seemed as if he were trying to avenge his younger brother's death by creating as much mayhem as possible. But finally, his reign of terror came to an end. The authorities, who had been tracking him for months, cornered him at last at Hell's Mouth with no escape path open to him.

So, what to do? Give himself up and end up suffering the agonies of being 'hung by the neck until he be dead' – there was no such thing as 'the drop' in the eighteenth century. Those hung died slowly in agony. The smuggler stood on the dark, brooding cliffs, below him the sharp treacherous rocks and the grey, raging sea, rolling in before a violent storm.

Defiant to the end, he gave one last shout and leapt off the edge. The last thing that was heard by the officers of the crown was one last bloodcurdling scream as he plummeted a precipitous 350ft onto the sharp, cruel rocks below. Some time later, watchers on the cliff top saw his poor, crumpled, lifeless body – until the sea claimed it for its own. He had at least cheated the hangman.

Now, on wild winter days, in dark and stormy weather, when the wind howls, and the sea dashes itself upon the rocks, legends have it that the cries and screams of the dead smuggler can still be heard. Anyone brave enough to stand on the high cliffs will wrap their coat about themselves and leave Hells Mouth and Dead Man's Cove to the elements and hurry away as fast as they can.

HELLS MOUTH AND DEADMAN'S COVE
ON THE NORTH COAST OF CORNWALL, WEST OR REDRUTH
OPEN ALL DAY – AND NIGHT TOO IF YOU'RE GAME

JAMAICA INN

Of Ghosts and Smugglers

Many years ago, a stranger stood at the old bar of the Jamaica Inn in Cornwall and quietly drank his ale. Shortly afterwards, he was called outside and he went to see what it was, leaving his beer on the counter. He never returned to finish his drink that day or any other day, for on the following morning, his murdered body was found on nearby Bodmin Moor.

Centuries upon centuries of haunting.

That might have been the end of it until, in 1911, there was a hubbub of mystery. The local press had received yards of correspondence. The interest here was of a strange figure, seen by many locals, sitting on the wall outside the Jamaica Inn. He didn't move or speak, even when openly addressed. But most of all, his appearance was uncannily like the murdered man. And on dark nights, when the wind howled and decent folk were well in bed, ghostly footsteps could be heard along the passageway of the inn, as the dead man's spirit came back to finish his pot of ale.

In his excellent little book, *Ghosts Around Bodmin Moor*, Michael Williams recalls a visit made by the Ghost Club Society in April 2001. The small bar produced another phenomenon. 'It was the strong whiff of pipe tobacco, nothing at all like a modern cigarette. Curiously, that smell went and later came back – as if confirming that supernatural forces were at work.'

Michael goes on to say that in 2004, TV's *Most Haunted* team said they were terrified by a night spent there. He cites visits by many others who have experienced supernatural happenings.

There are many unsolved murders – fact and fiction – on the lonely moor but one novel above all will be remembered: Daphne Du Maurier's *Jamaica Inn*. Who has better described Cornwall in November, the Jamaica Inn in the first chill of winter?

It was a cold, grey day in late November. The weather had changed overnight, when a backing wind brought a granite sky and mizzling rain with it, and although it was only a little after two o'clock in the afternoon, the pallor of a winter evening seemed to have closed upon the hills, cloaking them in mist.

The young author was inspired to write the novel when one day, riding over the moor, she became lost in a thick fog and sought refuge before a roaring fire in the inn. While recovering from her ordeal, the local rector is supposed to have entertained her with ghost stories and accounts of smuggling; he would later become the enigmatic figure of the vicar of Altarnun.

But was the Jamaica Inn really the centre of a smuggling ring as it appears? Circumstantial evidence points that way. The inn's village, Bolventor, was within easy reach of the coast, yet far enough away, so it could have been the ideal place for smuggling. It was something of a clannish business, with almost everyone in the community supporting it. One of the first Excise Units was based in Polperro, only fifteen miles away, but they were so badly received nobody would accommodate them so they were forced to live on a boat in the harbour.

But the Jamaica Inn is much older than that and we must go back in time to trace something like a beginning. Once upon a time, there were only tracks across the moor. Then in 1769, a turnpike road was laid and coaches rumbled across it taking their fares from London to Penzance and back again. A local woman, Mary Yellan, among the first to cross that atmospheric span of open country, describing what she saw, 'mile after mile of bleak moorland rolling like a desert land to some unseen horizon.' Well to put it in perspective, the moor actually stretches twelve miles north to south and eleven miles east to west. The route she took was roughly where the A30 winds its way today.

But the Jamaica Inn is even older than the first coaches. It was built in 1574, when it was known as the New Inn. It was later changed in honour of a man named Rod, a local squire. He held a government post in Jamaica and when he retired the inn was renamed in his honour.

Local man Reg Carthew has known the Jamaica Inn for some sixty years. Does he believe the inn was haunted? He replied in the affirmative and said that whenever he had to go to the old engine room and lifted his hand on the bolt on the door, he automatically looked behind him, feeling more than anything else a presence there, a sensation.

The crew of television's hugely successful series, *Most Haunted*, spent the night at the inn and the Ghost Society and LIVINGtv also paid a visit. As always with this programme, varied ghosties were found, including the malevolent figure of a highwayman in a tri-corned hat, and an anguished young mother and her baby. They also pinpointed areas in the inn which they claimed to be haunted. These include the new reception area (previously the boiler room), the Smuggler's Bar, the Stable Bar, and upstairs in bedroom four. The *Most Haunted* team claim to have located an American pilot, believed to be trying to find a photograph of his wife and child that he left at the inn.

Perhaps there is not one spooky episode that would make us conclude that the inn is haunted. But as Michael Williams points out, it is the accumulation of story after story, going back over the centuries that make up the old Inn's claim to fame.

JAMAICA INN
BOLVENTOR, CORNWALL, PL15 7TS
TEL: 01566 86250
OPEN AT THE PUBLIC AT THE APPROPRIATE TIMES

SIX

Cumbria

LEVENS HALL

The curse of the dying gypsy, the Little
Black Dog and other phantoms

A magnificent setting for its many ghosts, Levens Hall must be one of the finest Elizabethan houses in the north-west of England. It is full of treasures. Rooms are panelled with decorative plaster ceilings and contain fine furniture and many objets d'art. A family home, the Hall has been used for many television series, including *Haunted House*. Also on display is a harpsichord made by the late Robin Bagot which is still played at concerts in the Hall.

Levens Hall. (courtesy of Hal Bagot)

Leven's Hall – A happy arrangement with the family ghosts. (courtesy of Steve Bailey)

Levens Hall is perhaps best known for its world-famous topiary garden which was laid out in the late seventeenth and early eighteenth centuries. It was designed by Guillaume Beaumont who worked for Le Notre, responsible for the gardens at Versailles. Beaumont also worked for the British King James II, in whose court he undoubtedly met James Grahme, the then owner of Levens Hall.

Successive generations of the family have retained the gardens and park as Beaumont planned them and as such, are a rare example of their period. Beautiful spring and summer bedding, colourful herbaceous borders and lime walks surrounding a playing fountain, attract thousands of visitors each year.

The medieval defensive Pele Tower was the first building on the site and it forms the core of the Elizabethan mansion built by James Bellingham. The many occupants of the Hall have certainly left their mark on the creation of this house, and stories of legends and ghosts abound. The often seen Grey Lady is believed to be the ghost of a gypsy who was turned away from the house when she came begging for food. Before dying of starvation, she cursed the family living at Levens, saying 'no son should inherit the house until the River Kent ceased to flow and a very white fawn was born.'

True to her curse, the house passed through the female line for many generations. The birth of Alan Desmond Bagot in 1896 heralded the new era, for the river froze and a white fawn was found in the herd in the year he was born. Subsequent male heirs have always been born in deepest winter with ice on the river.

The gypsy, if this was indeed the 'Grey Lady', continues to haunt. Andrew, writing in the early 1970s, says that the ghost was seen by Lisa Bagot when she was seven in 1954 and again in 1971 when the figure was seen standing on a narrow bridge and 'nearly caused a motor accident'.

Andrew wrote that he met Annette Bagot in August 1972 when she told him that a party of Women's Institute members visiting Levens Hall saw another apparition, the Pink Lady – in a pink dress and mob-cap, as worn by servants. But like so many ghosts, her identity is unknown.

A male visitor belonging to another party of sightseers, complained that the family's black dog had pushed past him down the stairs and 'was a danger to the public'. But the Black Dog was no family pet and could not possibly have pushed anybody down the stairs, for the Black Dog was also a ghost, amorphous but ethereal. According to the present owner of the house, Mrs Susan Bagot, the Little Black Dog, as the creature is known, has been seen by many people. It can appear outside the house or inside running up the stairs. It then simply 'vanishes.'

Ghosts are also busy in the 'new' wing, built by Colonel Grahme in the late seventeenth century. Indistinct figures have been spotted and Susan Bagot told me that it can be 'very noisy and active'. Sleeping guests have been woken by the sound of unknown 'running footsteps and laughter'.

Susan Bagot says other sightings continue as successive generations inhabit this fine old mansion where so many generations have lived and died. She concludes that 'those who have gone before them live in companionable unity with each other.' Ghosts have almost become 'family.'

LEVENS HALL

NEAR KENDAL, CUMBRIA

TEL: 01539 9561346

SITUATED ON THE A6, 5 MILES SOUTH OF KENDAL

OPEN TO THE PUBLIC, SUNDAYS TO THURSDAYS

SEVEN

Devon

CHAMBERCOMBE MANOR

'Two little girl ghosts accompany me most days'

Chris Holloway of Chambercombe Manor, in Ilfracombe, says she feels the 'presence' of two little ghosts as she goes about her business. They don't worry her at all – certainly never scare her. Chris doesn't actually see the two girls, although they have been spotted in the upstairs rooms.

Their details, including their names, have been provided by a medium. The first girl is Rebecca (called Bella); she wears a blue dress, has light brown ringlets and sucks her thumb. The second girl, Alie, who died in what is known as the Chippendale Room, has short hair and is generally thought to have a 'sad look' about her.

Chambercombe Manor advertises itself as haunted and there are other spooks to substantiate the claim. A ghostly lady in a white dress has been seen in the vicinity of the pond behind the café. There are also several 'cold' spots in the house. The staircase which rises from the dining room to the Tudor Room has 'a decidedly unnerving atmosphere' – in consequence 'very few people like to go up these stairs. You feel as if somebody were trying to push you down stairs,' Chris told me.

The Tudor Room itself has its story. Once a long time ago, a little fourteen-year-old girl had a baby out of wedlock and her father was so furious and ashamed, he drowned the wee thing. Today, at times, the baby has been seen in its crib, wrapped in swaddling clothes. The young mother is at the end of the bed, crying.

Back in the 1980s when Andrew was researching Chambercombe Manor for his *Ghosts of Today*, he wrote about a 'secret room' in this eleventh-century building, not discovered until 1865. It had been completely walled up, including the window. It contained a four-poster bed, rotting curtains still drawn, and the skeleton of a young woman lying on the mattress. When the investigation failed to discover the cause of death or who she was, the remains were buried in the local churchyard. Today, the room is open for visitors. Chris told me that as part of their regular ghost tours, they show the room to the guests and tell its story.

A crown in this room has often been found to have moved onto the Jacobean chest and the candle put on the floor. It happens on anniversaries, often around September.

Andrew writes of other ghosts, but they were of those heard rather than seen. In an almost deserted building, footsteps could be heard walking the corridors of the manor and continued to the chapel and to the cobbled courtyard. 'Weird moans' were heard coming from the 'secret room.' Enough to give you the heebie jeebies really.

CHAMBERCOMBE MANOR
ILFRACOMBE, DEVON, EX34 9RJ
TEL: 01271 862624
OPEN TO GUESTS AT THE APPROPRIATE HOURS
OPEN TO GHOSTS AT ANYTIME

THE LORD HALDON COUNTRY HOUSE HOTEL

A faceless spectre, a monk buried alive and a drowned pregnant wench. Find them still if you dare

'There are places in the hotel where people just don't like to go,' Vikki Nicholls, the general manager of the Lord Haldon Country House Hotel, told me. 'There's a presence there. Something nasty. It's hard to explain.'

The hotel has had its fair share of grisly happenings, unexplained deaths and suicides. Both guests and staff have been treated to figures gliding by, the sound of smashing crockery in the dead of night, taps on bedroom doors at 3 a.m. and – incredibly – the very names of the frightened listeners called out.

Back in the early 1970s when Andrew was working on *Our Haunted Kingdom*, the name of the then guest house was simply Haldon House Guest House. He reported some of the darker happenings that had taken place within its old walls. One story concerned Sir Robert, later to become Lord Haldon. He fathered two sons who were continually fighting until one of them simply 'disappeared'. The records have been searched for the missing man but mention of only one son can be found. Perhaps the other son is still here: is it him perhaps that you find lurking along the corridor in the dead of night?

Former owners, Mr and Mrs Martin, treated Andrew to another story in November 1970. Their '300-year-old house' was haunted, they said, by the head and shoulders of a faceless figure which had been seen gliding past a ground-floor glass panel. This may be connected with the story of a monk who was buried alive here. But no-one knows where or when.

A Mrs Parmenter, who had an interest in the hotel, told Andrew that horses' hooves had been heard in the dead of night and that an unnamed 'apparition had been seen in the bar.'

And what of the girl's suicide I mentioned earlier? Vikki Nicholls had the story though she's unsure when the events took place. A maid in the house was courting one of the groomsmen and their intimacy resulted in the girl's pregnancy. Her lover would not have been the first man to duck responsibility in such circumstances. Desperate, the girl took what was perhaps the only way out known to her – she drowned herself. Her ghost has been seen here and there in the hotel – but especially in room thirty-four.

It was from this same room, number thirty-four, that another guest came down to breakfast one morning and jokingly said there must have been a ghost in his room the previous night. He said he had been woken up by the sound of cups and saucers on his tray smashing onto the floor. He may have joked. The staff knew different. They knew it was no joke. They knew.

THE LORD HALDON COUNTRY HOUSE HOTEL

DUNCHIDEOCK, NEAR EXETER, DEVON

TEL: 01392 832483

OPEN TO THE PUBLIC AT THE APPROPRIATE HOURS

4 MILES FROM EXETER, ABOUT 6 MILES FROM THE M5

ROYAL CASTLE HOTEL

Snow in the enclosed courtyard? Don't laugh.
It could be a resigning matter

Weird things happen in the Royal Castle Hotel at Dartmouth in Devon. Snow really has been seen and felt in an enclosed courtyard. Ghostly men have been witnessed fighting outside the hotel. And everyone here waits for October to come round. For it is then that the autumnal Coach and Horses can be heard (but not seen). It is thought that the ghost of Queen Mary, wife of William III, is in the carriage. Legend has it that the coach usually arrives around two in the morning – a sign of impending death. Apparently all this has been too much for more than one night porter; they have asked for their P45s and fled.

At the time I was writing this entry – it must have been in 2006 – the hotel's marketing manager, Emma Williams, rang to report two more ghostly incidents that had taken place in what they are now calling the Haunted Room. 'Last night a guest reported the feeling of someone actually sitting on the bed and then her bedclothes being pulled off,' Emma told me. The guest added: 'It was a bit of a tug-of-war for a while. Then whatever it was finally gave in.' A strong, determined woman, I thought, who would not play second fiddle for anyone, ghost or not.

While this bed-tugging was being discussed, another member of the hotel staff remembered a ghostly happening in the Haunted Room during 2005. A guest woke to see a figure looking over the bed. At first, in the half-dark, she thought it was her husband, but when she turned round she saw him sleeping the sleep of the just beside her. She then turned round again to look for the ghost, and 'it simply faded away.'

Andrew discovered a great deal more about this grand old hotel back in 1973. The hotel was built in 1584 and has a famous Lidstone iron cooking range made about 350 years ago. The present bar was formally two kitchens.

The ghost-hunter admired the genuine feeling of antiquity in the Adam dining room with its unusual staircase and magnificent view of the river. He cited a number of celebrities who have stayed in the hotel over time. These have included Sir Francis Drake, Charles II, Queen Victoria and Edward VII. Princess Margaret once travelled to the hotel to await her husband, Lord Snowden's, arrival. As it turned out, he had had a change of plans (he had landed at Torbay) and word was brought by courier around two in the morning. But nothing spooky there, I'm afraid.

ROYAL CASTLE HOTEL
11 THE QUAY, DARTMOUTH,
SOUTH DEVON, TQ6 9PS.
TEL: 01803 833033.
OPEN TO THE PUBLIC AT THE APPROPRIATE HOURS.

EIGHT

Dorset

THE CROWN HOTEL

The poltergeists are still busy at the Crown –
not to mention a ghost or two besides

In 1966, after a lot of conversion work had been carried out at the Crown in Poole, Dorset, Andrew discovered plenty of ghostly things to write about. He found disembodied voices, a tinkle on the piano in an empty room, doors open that had just been locked and the sound of something heavy 'being dragged' across the floor of an empty upstairs room. He also reports 'a misty figure gliding down the stairs.'

Now, some forty years later, things are still going haywire at the Crown, under the watchful eyes of Truda Clarke, the landlord's wife. Truda reports cutlery moving itself from tables, guests locked in their rooms, locked doors opening without a key,

Truda Clarke proundly shows off her hotel.

and keys themselves spinning in their sockets. A ghost in a Victorian nightdress has been seen. Another ghost 'with calming hands' has been felt – her invisible hands gently stroking a guest's hair (the spook was thought to be female). Truda told me that the editor of *Encounter* had seen a ghost in his room and was 'not frightened a bit'. (She thought it only fair not to give his name). There have been the sounds of children playing – when there were no children anywhere near.

Some guests, Truda told me, have been truly frightened. It was all too much for one couple who were so scared by a ghost in their bedroom, they said: 'no way are we staying!' A medium – who ought to be used to such things – swore that she would 'never, never come back', she had been so frightened.

There are several other things of interest belonging to the old building's history – it was once a thatched cottage dating from the seventeenth century, later to become a coaching inn. Sometime after it was built, the remains of two humpback twins were found chained together under what is now the larder. What cruel murderer so entombed them is unknown. It is also interesting that 'the hanging judge,' bloody Judge Jeffries, was a regular visitor here before holding court in Christchurch to condemn West County peasants captured after the Battle of Sedgmoor.

Watch your belongings.

NINE

East Sussex

BATTLE ABBEY

Monks galore!

Monks in black. Monks in brown. Monks arguing. Monks doing their utmost to scare the living daylights out of harmless visitors. And monks gently gliding through a convenient wall: Battle Abbey is full of them. The original abbey – on the site of England's greatest defeat – was built by William the Conqueror. Most parts of the buildings that survive today date from the thirteenth, fourteenth and fifteen centuries.

Battle Abbey. After seeing the photograph, Andrew saw a ghost here in front of one of the entrances. It is shown in white. (courtesy of the Andrew Green Archives)

The ghost walk at Battle Abbey. (courtesy of the Andrew Green Archive)

The original monks of the abbey were Benedictines whose habit was black (hence Blackfriars) but one, Robert de St Martin, left to form the first Cistercian abbey in nearby Salehurst in the thirteenth century and it was this group that wore white or light fawn clothing. Battle Abbey is now owned by English Heritage.

Andrew discovered several free spirits for his 1980 *Ghosts of Today* and more in his *Unknown Ghosts of the South-East*, published posthumously. The following account is a mixture of Andrew's experiences and what I have learnt from other sources.

On 30 April 2002, Jill Sutcliffe, a teacher at Sutton Valance School in Kent, was visiting the abbey with a school party of forty-five. It was about eleven o'clock when they were leaving the medieval undercroft. She had turned back to see if all her charges had emerged from the cellar when she saw 'apparently in rather a hurry and seemingly rather irritated by something' a grey-haired monk wearing a white habit with a prominent red belt. Jill said she was about to say hello, but felt he was far too busy.

When they arrived back at the shop, Jill enquired about their monk-in-a-hurry. Surely he was part of a film, a reenactment or something; she could hardly believe her ears to be told that their monk was simply one of the many ghosts seen about the abbey. In the same year, both Melanie Rudge and her daughter from Tingley in West Yorkshire, saw a monk near the old dairy.

In 2004, in the abbey's Novices Room, a photograph was taken of the fireplace. This showed a number of floating 'orbs' – sort of floating balls of lights which some people think of as the early stages of an apparition. Unfortunately, we've been unable to find either the photograph or its owner.

Another photograph – and this we do have – was taken in September 2001, and shows the ghostly figure of a man hanging from a doorway in the abbey. Is he hanging? Is it even a man? It's ghostly and hard to see. But look on page 51 and you can judge for yourself.

In the early 1990s, Stuart Dunkley from Zimbabwe took a photograph in the deserted cloister area at the back of Battle Abbey School. When the film was processed, a disembodied face was seen in a beam of light. Regrettably no copy of this photograph was kept at the abbey and there is no way to trace Stuart Dunkley.

Mrs Hazel Smith from Totton, Southampton visited the abbey on Thursday 29 June 2006. She saw not a monk, but a seat that could easily have been designed for monks to sit on, 'a stone seat set in an aperture near the stone stairway'. There is no seat of that description, or anything like it in the abbey. I suppose a stone seat may be seen as a kind of ghost.

Another view of the front of the abbey. (courtesy of the Andrew Green Archive)

Daryl Burchmore, one of the senior abbey custodians, told me of his own experience with the supernatural. In early 1990, at around 5.45 p.m., in the darkness of mid-winter, he was locking up in the undercroft for the night. Daryl was quite alone; all visitors had left. He went into the undercroft, which contains a series of chambers; he searched each one until he was sure everybody had gone. Then, on locking the outer door, out of the empty dark, he heard very loud knocking on the internal doors. Someone cried 'Let me out! Let me out!' Daryl quickly unlocked the door, only to find nobody there. He tore back to his colleagues in the shop and said he felt as if his heart was trying to burst out of his chest.

We now move back to the 1980s and the incident that so scared John Thomas. John was a maintenance man working in a trench connecting wires and cables to an old model of the Battle of Hastings. He suddenly realised that he was not alone in the dark undercroft. He saw that a monk was with him. Running out as if all the devils in hell were after him, he joined his colleagues. He refused to return to the building that night.

Going back another decade to the 1970s, a St Leonards' man, James Minahane, was visiting the abbey with his mother. He has left us the story that he suddenly realised there were two monks arguing nearby: one was dressed in white, the other in black. James too left in rather a hurry.

Probably the most startling photograph of a ghost at the abbey was taken by a parent of a pupil at the Battle Abbey School. Mr Lovett-Darby visited Battle Abbey in 1974 and took a photograph of his daughter in the common room. There was nobody else in the area at that time but the print clearly shows a mystery figure in the doorway leading through to the lower rooms of the main building.

Now let's see what Andrew unearthed for *Ghosts of Today*. He reckoned that there were at least three visible apparitions and two or more unseen walkers at the abbey. In 1972, in the huge common room, where real monks used to relax, a young lad saw a Norman knight standing in the corner nearest the Chapter House.

Two years later, an elderly man in a brown leather jerkin and apron, as worn by a farrier, was seen by another visitor in the same area. When the tourist asked one of the guides who the man was, she was assured that she was the only person to see the apparition. She had to be given treatment for mild shock.

Another sighting was that of a monk in a brown habit. This may well have been the same phantom taken to be a farrier in the previous sighting. It might also be the same figure as was seen on another occasion by Joyce Pain of Starrs Green.

Joyce said to Andrew: 'I was walking along the pavement beside the churchyard of St Mary's church one evening when, nearing my solicitor's office, I became aware of a figure moving along the pavement and gliding towards the gateway of the abbey. It was a monk in a dark habit but his face was hidden by the cowl. He continued for approximately ten yards before suddenly disappearing. She said: 'I was so utterly surprised that I could hardly believe I had seen a ghost. I certainly experienced no fear, only complete astonishment.'

Some time later Joyce became a secretary to the headmaster of the school in the Abbot's house, and there she had another, more mystifying experience: 'On this occasion I had to go up to the staff room,' she said, 'and because a class was in session, I chose to go through the Great Hall and up the main staircase. Halfway up the staircase, I suddenly heard a loud rustling exactly like that of a silk skirt. But there was absolutely no explanation for it. There was nobody there. I even walked into the alcove at the bend of the stairs, but it was empty, as was the staff room at the end of the corridor.'

Only a few feet away from this, in 1931, a small chapel was discovered – following a disastrous fire. This newly discovered room, 12ft by 16ft, still retains some of the original early plaster and signs of a wall mural. Shortly after the Second World War, the room was divided into two rooms, one of which is now a bathroom.

Joyce Pain had no explanation for footsteps associated with 'a lady in red', which have been heard previously on the stairs. We don't know the identity of the phantom but the suggestion is that she is intending to visit the chapel to complete her meditations.

A ghost seen in 1977 by Marcus Granger, a [then] well-known psychometrician, was of a woman dressed in a long red gown of the Elizabethan period. She appeared whilst one of the Webster family was conducting a group of visitors round the abbey. The figure just 'suddenly appeared in one corner of the room in which we were standing and after a few seconds, faded away.'

Andrew commented on yet another ghostly female who had been seen a few years previously. The lady appeared in a grey dress and walked along the corridor leading from the Great Hall to the Abbot's house. Her heavy, limping footsteps were also heard by a student at around 9.30 p.m. one night in September 1974.

Finally, there was one rumour Andrew wanted to debunk. There has never been – and Andrew believes there never will be – a ghost of King Harold with an arrow in his eye haunting the abbey, as some claim. Even though it would somehow complete the picture.

BATTLE ABBEY
BATTLE, EAST SUSSEX
TEL: 01424 773792
OPEN TO THE PUBLIC AT APPROPRIATE HOURS

THE HAUNTED MARRIAGE BED

Harry and Helen's new marriage was at breaking point. Helen was convinced they were haunted by Harry's late departed wife. She had seen proof of it with her own eyes – just what the ghost had done. The couple lived in a Brighton council flat and in desperation they asked the council if they could help. Could they? This was no everyday request. But one councillor had been a student in Andrew's popular night classes on the paranormal and it was this man who asked Andrew if he could investigate. Could it be a ghost, he wondered?

When Andrew called at the flat, the couple were full of the latest example of so called paranormal behaviour. The previous night, they had played a harmless game of Scrabble together. When they went off to bed, they left the Scrabble pieces on the carpet. They were too tired to put them away – or perhaps just too lazy. So far, so good. A blow like that of a steam hammer hit them both the next morning when they came down for breakfast. They were surprised and horrified to find that the scattered Scrabble pieces now formed one word. It was the name of Harry's recently deceased wife, Margaret. But it wasn't Margaret that was spelled out, but Harry's pet name for her. There it was, as sharp as a samurai sword. It was MAGGIE…

Helen was certain that she was being haunted by Margaret's ghost. And this was what they told Andrew when he came to see them. They had told the council they wanted a ghost-hunter and here he was. Andrew had long conversations with the couple and was convinced that this was no simple haunting. Helen was inordinately jealous of Harry's first wife and the incidents of psycho kinesis made her more so.

Andrew felt he knew what was going on, even if Harry and Helen didn't. To Andrew, it was as clear as daylight. This was no ghost trying to wreck their marriage. Helen had rearranged the Scrabble pieces herself – though it was clear she had no recollection of it. In a sleep-walk, in a trance – the sleuth didn't know – but somehow Helen was the cause of her own misery.

The solution was clear though drastic. Helen and Harry must remove everything associated with Margaret. It was the only way to lay the ghost for good, such as it was. 'That bed must go,' Andrew advised. 'And so must those small trinkets. They are all reminders of a past life. You must stop thinking about it.'

Reluctantly, painfully even, everything associated with Margaret was removed. After this major operation, Andrew paid them another visit. The now very happy couple had been able to put jealousy behind them. BBC Southern Counties Radio ran the story and quoted the leader of the council as saying, 'Andrew Green is the best marriage counsellor we've got.'

Andrew had always stressed to me that it wasn't only ghosts he found in his investigations. For Andrew, it often meant a trip to the client's GP, with, of course, the client's permission. An interview with the doctor often helped completely solve the problem. A client could claim he was hearing voices or any number of things. And it could be something as simple as the wrong medication or eating the wrong food with a particular programme of pills. For some sixty years, Andrew had helped people sort out their problems. But through it all, he had kept his feet firmly on the ground. He needed to.

ANDREW'S PRIVATE CASE
ANDREW CANNOT BE REACHED BY NORMAL METHODS OF COMMUNICATION

IDEN KENNELS

She looked up and saw a strange man beside her bed

It was about 1970, a year or so after the Fiddimore family had established what is now a highly reputable kennels, that they first saw their ghost. Mrs Sylvia Fiddimore was enjoying a cup of tea in her newly built kitchen, when a middle-aged man shuffled past the window. She opened the door to greet her visitor and was confronted with... nothing.

Now, nearly forty years later, the family is quite used to what they've come to know is a gamekeeper. He's stockily built, about fifty years old and wears what was originally thought to be a loose, fawn sweater with with – but now recognized as an old gamekeeper's smock. I spoke to Bernardine, the daughter of the house, who told me everyone is now quite used to the ghost. Sometimes, she looks up from the table – and there he is, just passing by the window. She said she had seen him twice this year already.

According to Andrew, writing in 1977, the Fiddimores are not the only ones to have witnessed the old gamekeeper. A friend of a friend, staying in a caravan in their garden, awoke one morning to find a strange man beside her bed. She didn't scream – for like everyone else who's seen the old gamekeeper, he 'created no fright, merely a feeling of warm friendliness and interest.' In this instance he glanced at the woman in bed, walked to the far end of the caravan and... 'vanished.'

But who was this ghost? Had he been a local? Early in 1979, after Jim Fiddimore had finished giving a talk on rabies to the Women's Institute, one of the ladies asked if she could visit their house. 'I lived there with my grandfather,' she explained. 'I would love to see the old place again. He was the gamekeeper there and always wore an old smock.' Of course the granddaughter came to visit.

She was sure it was her grandfather. The Fiddimores had their man.

IDEN KENNELS
KEEPERS COTTAGE, COLDHARBOUR LANE,
IDEN, EAST SUSSEX
TEL: 01797 230884
PRIVATE, PLEASE RESPECT

SEVEN STARS INN

The rage and fury of poltergeists

There appeared to be pandemonium in the cellar. 'It was as if a large crowd had just come in,' Christine Pierce told me, 'but I knew the pub was empty.' It was fortuitous that Andrew was with her – on one of his first cases involving a poltergeist. They went down to the cellar and it was empty. It was the early 1980s and Christine and her husband, Mike, had only recently taken over the licence of the Seven Stars pub in Robertsbridge.

On this particular occasion, Christine and Andrew retreated upstairs and once again, it sounded like mayhem had broken out down in the cellar. They went down to investigate for a second time but were unprepared for what awaited them in the usually well-kept and tidy cellar. There were bottles everywhere and one of the larger kegs was deeply wedged into a recess. That alone would have needed the strength of a superman.

The next time the poltergeist struck – for by this time Christine realised what it was – she was by herself, having a quiet cup of coffee in one of the back rooms. She told me the noise was similar to what it had been before – as though a lot of folk were simply whooping it up down there.

Christine bravely unlocked the door leading to the cellar. The noise stopped as she went in. But what a difference! She had left a pile of the freebies, Friday Ads, neatly tied in a bundle with secure nylon tape. The tape was still there but it held nothing.

Left: *The legendary 'Red Monk' of Robertsbridge in the Seven Stars.*

Right: *The haunted corridor. At the far end a steep, narrow stairway leads to a loft and a mysterious 70ft deep shaft.*

Left: *Bedroom affected by poltergeist activity.*

Right: *Site of the witnessing of the figure of a monk in 1471.*

Copies of the magazines were scattered to the four winds. By this time, Christine was more annoyed that scared. (The incident was reconstructed in the last of the 2002 television series, *Strange but True*. It was presented by Michael Aspel and showed Andrew 'in action'.)

There were others involved in the haunting. A self-styled 'psychic' and osteopath visited the pub and told Christine he felt a 'presence' there, and to add to the atmosphere at the time, the hair of Christine's dog was standing on end. The psychic osteopath was, like Andrew, reassuring and confirmed that a ghost will never harm you but, surprisingly, 'it will stand guard and protect you and your family.' Thankfully, Christine was easily reassured and she said that she was no longer afraid.

But the haunting didn't stop. The next time the kitchen was affected and there were several people there to witness the mayhem. A lamp exploded off its fastenings, cups flew across the room smashing against the walls and in another room, glasses levitated off their shelf, lamps smashed, and pot plants moved across the hearth from one side to the other. There was general chaos.

When the author, Guy Lyon Playfair, was interviewing Christine in the kitchen for his latest book, *The Haunted Pub Guide*, he was suddenly hit by a loaf of bread thrown several feet across the room by an invisible force.

On another occasion, Christine had a couple staying in what was called the Pink Room, and before having an afternoon nap, they left a jar of Marmite on the table. They awoke to find smears of Marmite spread all over the room. It was sickening.

The haunted 'Seven Stars' Inn in Robertsbridge, Sussex – reputed home of the ghostly 'Red Monk'.

Andrew had a theory as to what had caused these extraordinary happenings in the Seven Stars pub. The building, he explained, 'acts like a kind of video player and certain people at certain times seem to be able to press an invisible "Play" button for the action to begin.'

It's difficult to know which people cause poltergeist phenomena, termed psycho kinesis by experts and psychical researchers. A common theory is that a youngster at puberty – boy or girl – is unknowingly providing the energy that sets off the often terrifying chaos. Insurance claims are being considered. For example, Commercial Union told Andrew that they will consider claims arising out of poltergeist damage – but they are reluctant to publicise this.

In Andrew's 1997 *Haunted Sussex Today*, he discovered more activity in the Seven Stars. In July 1996, one of the bar staff told Andrew that 'a blackboard used as a menu moved from a shelf and tapped him on the shoulder. 'It didn't just fall, it moved,' he insisted.

Other members of staff had more stories. Jason Chaston reported that gas taps on the barrel had been turned off three times in one week 'by themselves.' Jane Syrett was not a little alarmed when a jelly on a shelf in the larder adjoining the kitchen, flew across the room and landed beside her. 'That's about 7ft it must have travelled all by itself,' she said.

In 1980, when Mrs McCarthy was in residence at the Seven Stars, something even more alarming took place. She had sent her son to her sister's house in St Albans for the weekend, hoping to ease the tension that had developed because of his forthcoming school examinations. She was not a little annoyed to find that her son's sheets had a large hole cut, badly, with a pair of scissor.

With mounting fury, she rang her son but knew him well enough to believe him when he said it wasn't him who had caused the damage. Mrs McCarthy bought two new sheets, put them on the bed, and locked the door. It's hard to imagine her feelings when the next day she found the new sheets had received similar treatment – large holes cut right through the tough plastic wrappings.

It is interesting to note that precisely the same thing happened to Christine Pierce, in her son's bedroom – two new pairs of sheets with large jagged holes cut in both of them.

Early in 1996, the new owner, Colin MacGregor, held a house warming and among the guests were two policemen from London. When the party finished, it was really too late for the policemen to catch their train back to London so their host put them up in the main sitting room, above the bar. They were woken by the sound of loud banging and to their amazement, saw two drawers of a Victorian dressing table rapidly open and close on their own accord. Andrew writes that the two policemen hid under their blankets. Surely not!

I asked the present owner, Mark Fox, for his experience in the five years or so that he has been at the Seven Stars and it seems that the haunting continues. His dogs, who will normally go anywhere, balk at entering the cellar. A guest had to constantly get out of bed to close a window that kept opening of its own accord. A friend found it impossible to get up from his bed for some time. He felt some force of the supernatural pushing, pushing him down.

For all its devils, the Seven Stars is an interesting old building, and dates from around 1187. In his 1973 *Our Haunted Kingdom*, Andrew notes that one of the rooms in the hotel was where King Charles I was reputed to have been kept prisoner. The book also says that a 70ft deep shaft runs from the loft to the cellar. In 1567 it was the only house to be held on the demesne of the Manor and is the largest and most elaborate of the existing medieval buildings in this attractive village.

Ruth Parkes, wife of the licensee in Andrew's time, told him that her two large Labradors had watched something unseen in her sitting room from the narrow corridor leading to King Charles' minute room.

And so the stories continue about this deeply interesting, severely haunted old pub. It is interesting to note that a survey by Tony Cornell and Alan Gould for their book, *Poltergeists*, found that some 25 per cent of poltergeists are place centred. That would be news to nobody at the Seven Stars.

SEVEN STARS INN
HIGH STREET, ROBERTSBRIDGE, EAST SUSSEX
TEL: 01580 880333.
OPEN AT APPROPRIATE HOURS

TEN

Essex

HADSTOCK CHURCH

Digger the dingo always made a beeline for the phantom's grave

'There he was, tail wagging and ears back', said Miss Croxton-Smith, fifty years resident of Hadstock in Essex, 'as though he were greeting a friend, hurrying into the church towards Carr's grave'. The Revd John Addison Carr was rector at St Botolph's Saxon church from 1786 until his death in 1836. The rector's ghost has been seen in or near the church here, but no one knows why Digger the dingo acts as he does.

During the research for *Ghosts of Today*, Andrew visited this lovely village, just over the border from Cambridgeshire. It was in this church, late in 1978, he writes, that Mrs Lettice Dawson, Digger's owner, saw the figure of a tall man in dark grey clothing walk silently down the aisle, turn as if to enter the vestry – and vanish. This doesn't sound at all like Carr. Apparently the Revd Carr was a short, bearded man, usually wearing a black cassock. His unmarked grave is at the foot of the chancel steps.

That was not the only time that a ghost has been seen. Miss Croxton-Smith has heard phantom footsteps in the empty church. She also mentions a young couple who left the church in a hurry one night and said an elderly gentleman had been very cross and turned them out. Of this, she says 'we can only speculate as to the reason the normally benign Carr was angry!' If it was him.

HADSTOCK CHURCH
HADSTOCK, ESSEX
ON B1052
NORMALLY OPEN TO THE PUBLIC

ELEVEN

Gloucestershire

PRESTBURY

Second most haunted village in England

Perhaps the best authority on the ghosts of Gloucestershire's Prestbury is Florence Jackson, now in her nineties, author of *Walking in Haunted Gloucestershire* and other books. As she has written more recently than Andrew, I'll deal with her ghosts first. And there are quite a number. She emphasised that she never accepted a ghost story unless it had been told her by two independent witnesses.

I'll start as she does, with The Burgage, the oldest street in the village and the scene of many hauntings. Situated half way along the street is Prestbury House, occupied for a short time during England's Civil War by Cromwell's men.

They knew that the Royalists were camped on Cleve Hill above the village. They also knew that the enemy was seriously in need of support. Desperate, they would need to get a message through to Gloucester, and the courier's route lay directly through Prestbury. Quietly, the soldiers laid a trap. They stretched a taut rope across the street and when the Cavalier came galloping along his horse stumbled and fell. Rider and dispatches were now in enemy hands.

Nowadays, people living in The Burgage still hear the horse and rider. They told Florence Jackson that they hear the galloping animal, the clatter of stumbling hooves, a short silence, and then the riderless horse forever racing into the night. A skeleton found nearby is believed to be that of the Cavalier, executed on the spot after his horse fell.

Others living in The Burgage still hear the stamping and snorting of horses in the night and a light 'which goes around the bedroom as if somebody is shining a lamp' but there is no one to be seen outside. Two sisters who lived near the crossroads where Mill Street joins The Burgage were determined to see the horse they had so often heard. At the sound of the galloping spectre, they dropped whatever they were doing and dashed outside. But they never saw anything and said simply that they 'felt' the horse gallop past them in the street.

Prestbury House is now a hotel, but from 1607 until 1964 it was owned by the Capel family. Shortly before the Second World War, some Scots visited the village.

They had heard that there was a pony for sale which they wanted for their ten-year-old daughter. The girl waited while her parents were negotiating, but bored by the grown-up talk, she wandered off to the old stables near Mill Street.

She was delighted to see a street party with lots of people dressed like those in a Jane Austen novel. She raced back to her parents with the urgent plea, 'Mummy, Mummy, come and see the fancy-dress party!' After trying to ignore the child for some time, Mummy eventually agreed to come. When they arrived at the spot, the girl could clearly see the party but her mother could see nothing. She scolded her daughter 'for making up fairy tales'.

But the child never forgot what she saw and thirty years later she again visited Prestbury. Research revealed that a famous grotto had existed in the eighteenth and nineteenth centuries – on the spot where she had seen the merry party. To publicise the Grotto, the advertisements read: 'The nobility, Gentry and company at Cheltenham may be accommodated with Breakfasts, Dinners and Tea at the short-est notice.' The records show some of the rich and famous who visited here.

On the opposite side of the Burgage is Sundial Cottage. The full story is unknown but the broad outline is that a young girl was forbidden to marry the man she loved and was confined to her room where she sought solace in playing the spinet. On quiet summer evenings when windows are open and all is at peace, the gentle sound of music can still be heard, wafting along the Burgage.

There is more to this story. During the Second World War, a mother and her twelve-year-old son fled the London bombs and came to live in Sundial Cottage. After a short time, the boy became irritable, off his food and generally looked unhappy. After persistent questioning from his mother, he finally blurted out, 'I can't sleep because of the funny music.' Puzzled, the mother exchanged bedrooms and she too heard 'the funny music'. It was only then that she heard the story about the spinet.

Walk, as Florence Jackson did, along Tachley Lane into Deep Street and you'll find a house called Three Queens – from where strange, inexplicable sounds are sometimes heard. Opposite the Three Queens is a bungalow and a thatched bakery. Occupants in both these houses report a hurrying monk who appears from time to time.

From here, there are three stone cottages – the middle one is believed to be haunted. The story goes that a four-year-old boy refused to stay in the kitchen when his mother went upstairs. He didn't like the soldiers who came in, he told his mother. 'What soldiers?' his mother asked. 'Funny soldiers with boots up to here', he said. pointing to his thigh – 'and with big hats.' Not a bad description for a four-year-old.

The lad was a newcomer to Prestbury and too young to know that a skirmish had taken place outside his house during the Civil War and that the thatched cottage opposite bears the scars of the characteristic spherical lead balls used commonly by both sides in the Civil War.

Prestbury Crossways, where the galloping Cavalier is heard. (courtesy of Florence E. Jackson)

Not far from this is the Reform Cottage. This house and garden are regular haunts of the Black Abbot, seen by many people at Christmas, Easter, and All Saints Day. Shortly before the Second World War, a Mr and Mrs Cousins moved in to the Reform Cottage. They grew accustomed to the regular ghostly visits but after the death of Mr Cousins, the family sold the house to a young couple from London. They told Ms Jackson that they were soon aware of a 'presence.' This didn't worry them much until they had some major alterations carried out. One of the workmen complained that 'there was always someone watching him'.

At the completion of the work, client and builder went over the plans and checked that everything was in order. They took little notice of the heavy plant encased in macramé that was attached to the ceiling. Suddenly, it began to swing violently. Then it crashed to the floor between them, missing the men by inches. Later they reasoned that the ghosts of the altered house didn't like the building they had done. 'But for the moment', the owner said, 'I've never seen three grown men crash downstairs quite so quickly.' He admitted that they were 'all very badly shaken.'

Not far from the Reform Cottage is St Mary's church. Here the Black Abbot walks down the aisle. He is supposed to have been exorcised – but he still appears. A former vicar saw him sitting on top of a table top tombstone. 'As I went over to him,' he said, 'he faded away in front of my eyes.'

From here, take the few steps down Mill Street. Opposite The Plough, pause for a minute, for this is the place where the Black Abbot has been seen early in the morning. This was once the farmyard of Church Farm. During the Second World War, a land girl arrived for work about 6 o'clock one morning, looking frail and frightened, saying she had seen the Black Abbot on the steps. With their seventh sense, animals seem to 'know' that something unfriendly is lurking nearby. Horses, and sometimes dogs, refuse to pass this spot.

Jock, a former postman, used to come here early in the morning with his bag. Stable boys from the nearby racing stables also exercised their horses here. Hearing them coming down Mill Street, Jock would always give a cheery 'Hello' and the lads would answer. But at other times, Jock would hear the phantom horses and stable boys. They were not to be seen nor did anybody answer his greeting.

There are many other uncorroborated ghost stories in Prestbury – it's not known as our second most haunted village for nothing. The village's most famous ghost – I've mentioned him several times in this entry – is the Black Abbot. Many people seeing a monk may take him for just that, a flesh and bone monk in his habit. Locals say 'he looks so real you may see him and not take him for a ghost at all.'

Most of the above was given me by Florence Jackson. Prestbury is Ms Jackson's home village so that does give her an advantage. Back in Andrew's *Our Haunted Kingdom*, he found six ghosts, all but one reiterated here by Ms Jackson.

Andrew also found Cleve Corner, a seventeenth-century farmhouse. There was a murder here in one of the bedrooms and some of those who've slept here have felt fingers around their throat. Like other ghosts we've described in this book, the ghost can manifest itself as 'a dim mysterious light'. And with this, there is a 'cold clamminess and a feeling of diabolical evil.' Tradition has it that the murderer killed a newly wed bride in her bedroom and stole all the wedding presents.

And that about covers Prestbury, Britain's second most haunted village. Perhaps it reflects what a really diligent researcher can do. And as for the number one haunted village – well, Pluckley once was; today the title is up for grabs. Great Livermere, in Suffolk, might just rank.

PRESTBURY VILLAGE
GLOUCESTERSHIRE
GHOSTLY STREET SITES ARE OF COURSE OPEN TO THE
PUBLIC, BUT PLEASE RESPECT PRIVATE HOUSES.

ST MARY'S CHURCH

More walks through walls

To ghost-hunters and the like, phantoms that look as solid as you or me, that can walk through walls, are almost commonplace. But to an ordinary member of the public, to witness such things is mindblowing. The Revd David Ackerman of St Mary's church at Kempsford, Gloucestershire, told me of just such a happening that took place in his church comparatively recently.

It happened in 1996 when a lady parishioner was busy cleaning the church and waiting for a friend to join her. It was about 4 p.m. and she saw a woman – a stranger to her – walk from one side of the church to the other. At a distance she could be mistaken for her friend – until this extraordinary thing happened. There in front of her, as cool as you like, this woman did in fact walk through the thick church wall. The friend arrived some minutes later, and by this time, the witness was in a slight state of shock.

Mr Ackerman was also anxious to tell me of a ghostly local legend. The garden of the Old Vicarage occupies part of the grounds of the old manor house. This includes a section of the terrace walk, parallel to the river, known as Lady Maud's Walk. This is so called owing to the story in which Lady Maud haunts the terrace. She is forever waiting for the return of her young brother, Henry, who was drowned in the river below. She is a patient ghost, for the last sighting was in the 1980s.

This Gloucestershire village of Kempsford lies on the banks of the Isis, or River Thames, whichever you prefer, and next to the very modern RAF Fairford. The unusual and attractive church, dedicated to St Mary, has a magnificent central tower with heraldic associations to the Duchy of Lancaster (the first duke was born in the castle).

Andrew writes that a few yards away from the church is the attractive sixteenth/seventeenth Old Vicarage which ceased being a working vicarage in 1980. It is a large building with several rooms once used as servant's quarters for, like many priests' houses, it has housed numerous varied characters and has seen a lot of changes. It is believed it was once a school, but whether this is connected with the three apparitions that have been seen here is not yet known. It was Andrew again who reported several odd experiences: one was an unusual noise coming from the stairway leading to the servant's quarters, another was the figure of a woman, wearing seventeenth-century dress, and carrying a baby, seen 'gliding down the stairs.' A third was a young boy in a blue suit, also seen 'on the stairs'.

ST MARY'S CHURCH
KEMPSFORD, GLOUCESTERSHIRE.
OPEN TO THE PUBLIC AT THE APPROPRIATE TIMES.

TWELVE

Hampshire

BEAULIEU ABBEY

The stately ghosts of Beaulieu

The stately home of Beaulieu has been owned by the same family since 1538 and is still the private home of the Montagus. It houses the famous National Motor Museum and rather a lot of ghosts, mostly monks as a matter of fact. Beaulieu Abbey was founded in 1204 when King John gave the land to the Cistercians. But in one sense, these Cistercian monks have never left. For, as Andrew says in *Our Haunted Kingdom* – and it still applies today – reports of more phantom monks bring little comment from Lord Montagu or his staff. What is perhaps surprising is that with so many ghosts around, Lord Montagu has never witnessed one. (Andrew saw four ghosts – in various places – in his entire lifetime).

Most of the ghosts at Beaulieu Abbey seem to be monks.

On summer nights, a ghostly Gregorian chant from the abbey echoes across the lawns.

At times, the spirits release a strong smell of incense.

This is no recent phenomenon. Ghosts have been seen, heard and sensed here for more than a hundred years. That's as far as the records tell us, but it is thought that such ghostly manifestations go back a lot longer than that.

One keen observer was the Revd Robert Frazer Powles, the vicar of Beaulieu from 1886 to 1939, and the monks were part of his daily life. He knew his ghosts by name, making comments like 'Brother Simon was here again last night. I heard his boots squeak.' Once a parishioner remarked to him that a service had been poorly attended but Powles retorted that it had in fact been very full, obviously counting the many ghost monks that only he could see.

At times of crisis – signalling a death in the village or imminent danger to one of the Montagus – the spirits that watch over the estate release a strong smell of incense, still in common use in churches by 'the old religion'. The aroma is strongest in the upstairs rooms that were once chapels.

It seems that most homes of active ghosts can produce at least one lady, white or grey. Beaulieu has its Grey Lady. She is generally thought to be Isabella, Countess of Beaulieu, who died in 1786 and whose portrait is on display. She has been seen several times walking through walls and making a lot of noise in what are now the private apartments of Palace House. Visitors have also seen her in the main house, taking her to be one of the staff. 'Why won't the costumed guide speak to us?' they ask.

Often thought to be another omen is the sound of a Gregorian chant, like the one used in services. You hear the sounds in the abbey, on some nights, and it echoes across the lawns. The chant can be quite loud, fade, and then resume at full strength. On one occasion, a resident, knowing that somebody had died, asked if a special service was being held for the departed. No, she was told. It was just the ghostly monks again.

Footsteps have been heard approaching the monastic doorways and climbing the stairs in the abbey at a time when only the observer was present. There is also the clink of keys with nobody there to hold them. A phantom funeral has been heard in the monks' burial ground, with the echo of slow footsteps, followed by the sounds of a spade in the earth.

Andrew reported one sighting in 1965 when a lady visitor saw the shadow of a monk 'in a brown habit seated in a recess just west of the magnolia, reading what looked like a scroll of parchment.'

We know that the monks arrived in 1204 and stayed till the Dissolution in 1538. Andrew wrote of the atmosphere of wellbeing these monks must have created with their hard work, sheep farming and agricultural pursuits. He went on to say that 'because of the general peace and tranquillity of Beaulieu, it is not really surprising that some of the early inhabitants remain – even though they are now mere phantoms.'

I hear you, Andrew. I hear you.

BEAULIEU ABBEY
BEAULIEU, HAMPSHIRE, SO42 7ZN
TEL: 01590 612345
OPEN TO THE PUBLIC AT THE APPROPRIATE HOURS

THIRTEEN

Hertfordshire

HOLLYBUSH PUBLIC HOUSE

Buried alive in a plague pit

Imagine the horror of being chucked into a plague pit and buried alive during the Great Plague of 1664-1665. All around you the lumps, the swellings, the suppurating pustules, amongst those who'd suffered the agony of a lingering death. This was the alleged fate of a fourteen-year-old girl, who now visits the Hollybush pub in Elstree as a ghost. Think of her as you park your car, for that is the place where she slowly died.

In the downstairs bar area there is a large fireplace with an ancient, wooden cross beam that was once, it is believed, part of the gallows in the infamous Newgate Prison. One of the unfortunate felons who died there now inhabits the Hollybush bar.

Back in Andrew's *Ghosts of Today*, he tells the story of previous landlords, a Mr and Mrs Cadell. Mr Cadell had recently retired from the Royal Navy and was used to tales of ghost ships at sea. He was nevertheless a sceptical man and reluctant to believe that the Hollybush was haunted – that was until an evening when both he and his wife heard footsteps on the empty stairs. 'They were slow and heavy like a man's footsteps,' he said.

Still pondering as to the cause of this unusual incident, Mrs Cadell heard the footsteps again. Going to investigate, she saw something that seemed to almost stop her heatbeat. Over the banisters, at the top of the stairs, she saw the head of a man, 'just like the old Van Dyke advertisement. He glanced down towards me, and then faded away,' she said. 'I yelled for my husband, but by then of course it was too late.' The mysterious bearded character was seen again nearly a year later by a member of staff.

The pub is a delightful old building dating from around 1451. It once boasted a tunnel, the entrance of which was hidden by a door in the bar – but nobody seemed know to where it led. The new manager, who took over towards the end of 2006, is Dean Hale. When I spoke to him, he'd apparently been there only a few months, not long enough perhaps to meet the resident ghosts. 'Not yet,' he emphasised. Ghosts unfortunately seem to reappear when least expected.

HOLLYBUSH PUBLIC HOUSE
HIGH STREET, ELSTREE, HERTFORDSHIRE
OPEN TO THE PUBLIC DURING APPROPRIATE HOURS.
TEL: 02082 076123

BROCKET ARMS

More monks (and how about a ghost of Bernard Shaw?)

Andrew, writing in the early 1970s, claims to have found when the Brocket Arms' ghost first appeared – about 9 p.m. early in 1969. A Mrs Sweeney was the witness. She was carrying some sandwiches through the dining room when she saw: 'a man dressed all in brown in a monk's outfit with a cowl and everything. His head was bent over so I couldn't see what he looked like. But as I turned to face him, he vanished.'

On a cold grey morning, some nine months later, he was seen again and this time we have a description – 'an old emaciated face in a sort of smokey haze, in the doorway of the dining room.'

As usual, there are various ideas as to how the monk died. Did he commit suicide, and if so, why? Another theory is that he had got a young member of the church pregnant. And the penalty for this was death. He was hung outside the pub (or was it inside?) – and earned the title for being the last man to be hanged in the village. Margery Waters, a cleaner at the pub, said she had seen, 'a mysterious grey figure walking in and out of the pub.' Weird noises were also heard.

In 1940, a poem was written which is displayed in the bar. The verse relevant to the hanging is as follows:

A monk had ridden as he fled from the mob
O howling villains who feared no god

They slung him up to a beam in the bar
Declaring he should not have ridden so far

73

Brocket Arms.

The Brocket Arms was built about 1378 and for many years was a hostelry for pilgrims. According to the records, there was not one but two girls who came to sticky ends at the Brocket Arms. We know the story for one poor wretch, but not the other. The story is typical and must have happened all over the country. First the girl was seduced by the son of the manor house: she was then locked in the pub cellar and 'foully done away in the fields beyond.'

Another pub ghost is a jovial priest, tried and hanged. Apparently, there is a priest hole on top of the fireplace, which should quickly remind the poor sinner of the fires of hell!

There are even those who claim to have seen the ghost of Bernard Shaw. Shaw lived locally at Shaw's Corner, from 1906 until 1950. According to Andrew there is yet another ghost at Shaw's Corner and this is Lawrence of Arabia, in life, a frequent visitor. Take your pick.

BROCKET ARMS
AYOT ST LAWRENCE, HERTFORDSHIRE, AL6 9BT
TEL: 01438 820250.
OPEN TO THE PUBLIC AT THE APPROPRIATE TIMES

FOURTEEN

Isles of Man & Wight

CASTLE RUSHEN

When hairs rise on the back of your neck and the dog
refuses to go in, that's the time to look for ghosts

A lot has happened in Castle Rushen since Andrew's *Ghosts of Today* was published in 1980 – and perhaps the best person to give you this recent ghostly information is the former custodian of the castle, Iain McKinlay (now retired).

Castle Rushen. (Courtesy of Manx National Heritage Museum)

Castle Rushen. (courtesy of Manx National Heritage Museum)

The main focus of activity has been in Derby House (Iain's flat), in the vicinity of the circular staircase, by the Deemster Room (robing room). During the 1980s and early 1990s, a woman's voice could sometimes be heard saying 'You are jealous,' in a French accent. I have heard no explanation for this.

In the early 1990s, a lot of building work was carried out in Iain's flat. This meant that his two young children had to play a game of musical beds, occupying different rooms on different nights. One evening, when Iain passed the room he thought his young son was in, he heard a distinct 'boo' as he went past. He only found out later that that room was unoccupied.

His young daughter often saw 'a smiling, shining lady' at the foot of her bed. The family later learned from the previous custodian that his son had also seen the lady. Apparently, the children had not been scared by these nocturnal visits – and the lady was only visible to children.

On another occasion, Iain reported having 'a waking dream' while in the bath. It concerned a young girl called Rose whose family had been in service in the castle. The girl suffered from an infectious disease and had been sent to Laxey by fishing boat. The boat reached its destination but Rose didn't. It was whispered that Rose had been thrown from the boat and that her spirit walked abroad. Had Rose tried to communicate with him? Had she really been thrown overboard?

Still in the 1980s, a lot of electrical work was carried out in the castle and the electrician reported that every now and then, he received a very positive tap on the shoulder from behind. Further, he suspected that he must have come up against a mischievous ghost for – normally a careful workman – his tools would somehow manage to be in a different place from where he had left them. It might be a pair of pliers, an electrician's screwdriver or something else.

Then there was the door with a mind of its own. A member of staff had gone into the guard room but couldn't get out again: it felt as if somebody, some thing was holding the door from the other side. He stepped back, let go of the door, and – hey presto – the door opened by itself.

Spooky things just kept on happening. An official group was being taken round the castle and were being shown a video. Without anybody touching it, the door of the video room was violently flung open, hitting the director who stood at the back of the room. These were small matters in themselves, but taken together they made the staff rather unnerved.

The Ammunition Room, known for its darker-than-normal shadows, is also unnaturally cold. The door has a tendency to either stick, or it forces itself back on you. A chilling experience occurred at the end of last season. In the gathering dusk, two of the younger members of staff went upstairs to lock up. They returned in a state of absolute terror, and to this day have not reported what they experienced.

Back in the winter of 2002-3, a member of staff was engaged in painting the seventeenth-century banqueting room when a young girl appeared, as if out of nowhere. The child was about ten years old with lank hair, blue eyes, bare dirty feet and wearing a Hessian cloth dress; she was generally dishevelled. The staff member said he could sense her before he turned round and took a better look. The ghost – for this is what she must have been – was there one minute and gone the next.

The same staff member, taking a group around the castle in the same area, was suddenly disturbed by the rattling of chains – the sound apparently coming from inside the walls. Much as the guide denied it, the group were convinced that the chain-rattling had simply been put on for their benefit.

The castle had its share of Doubting Thomases and one day, one of these went up the outside steps to the seventeenth-century room. He put his fleece on a chair, which promptly disappeared! His fleece fell on the floor. Rumour has it that he's a lot less sceptical of the castle goings-on these days.

There was some building work going on when a young child visited the castle with her family; she pointed to a woman standing on the scaffolding next to a

There has been a ghostly activity in this dramatic castle since Andrew's day. (courtesy of Manx National Heritage Museum)

figure of the builder. This is now an open courtyard but in the nineteenth century it was part of a prison and the area was built up and enclosed. The room seen by the child used to be the ground floor buttery.

Sightings of a lady – white, black, grey – are almost common in old buildings. On this occasion, Iain McKinlay, the custodian, was near the drawbridge on a winter's evening around dusk, when he saw a human-shaped/human-sized column of mist walk across the drawbridge and disappear through the black gates.

Another of Iain's reports concerns a local man drinking at the Castle Arms, adjacent to the castle. He stepped out of the pub into a rain-lashed, bleak, stormy night, when he saw a woman in black coming towards him. He was on the point of making a comment about the foul weather when she walked straight through the locked gates of the castle.

Castle guides have always referred to the underground area as a strange, spooky dungeon, because it is dark and dank, and this is what people expect and like. In reality it was originally the mill for the castle. But in the nineteenth century, the area was used as a prison by the local police. Prisoners were held here if they arrived after the main town prison had been locked up for the night.

In *Ghosts of Today*, Andrew points out that a large number of executions have taken place within the castle walls and that one of those judicially killed is now a phantom – that of an innocent woman hanged for murdering her son. But Andrew says her son died of natural causes. He reports that one of the guides saw the figure of a woman in a long grey dress with a young boy – seen standing near the drawbridge.

In *Our Haunted Kingdom*, Andrew cites others, like the wife of the warden who saw the apparition twice. On the first occasion, the ghost disappeared through the castle wall near the drawbridge when spoken to, and also a couple of years later when seen in the passage.

Andrew quotes a Mr Gale who had some knowledge of the affair. He says: 'The story of this mysterious lady was going on years before this and will probably continue for many years to come.' He continues, 'Although I have never seen this ghost, I find it hard to disbelieve all the people who have seen her through the years.'

In 1960, a group of young adolescents handed the curator a signed statement reporting details of the woman they had seen when the castle was empty and locked. She had appeared at the top of the Eagle Tower.

CASTLE RUSHEN

CASTLETOWN, ISLE OF MAN

OPEN TO THE PUBLIC AT THE APPROPRIATE HOURS

TEL: 01624 648000

WITH THANKS TO THE MANX NATIONAL HERITAGE MUSEUM,

DOUGLAS, IM1 3LY, FOR THEIR GENEROUS HELP AND CO-OPERATION.

BRADING THE EXPERIENCE

Who killed Lonely Louis?

Imagine an Isle of Wight hostelry some time during the Stuart period. The night is dark and Louis de Rochefort, believed to be a French agent assigned to make contact with King Charles I, then imprisoned at Carisbrooke Castle, is preparing for bed. He has been given a good dinner and shown to his room on the first floor, overlooking Quay Lane. He is too tired to mind the raucous din downstairs where there is a noisy gathering of seamen, prostitutes, gamblers, thieves and riff-raff of all kinds. He soon drops into a deep sleep.

Louis de Rochefort doesn't hear the intruder creeping up the stairs to the first floor. Nor does he hear the assassin noiselessly crossing the floor where the Frenchman is sleeping. There is no hesitation from this determined killer. In goes the knife into the sleeping form, once, twice, three times. The knife penetrates deeply into the body. The man dies fairly quickly, but not before his screams pierce even the hubbub downstairs. It is said that with his dying breath, he cursed his murderer and swore to haunt the building until his remains were returned to his homeland and given a proper burial there. The deed was done and the murderer vanished. What remained was the spirit of the murdered man, his ghost if you like?

Brading – where the deed took place – is a small town on the Isle of Wight and speculation went wild in the week following the killing. What sort of man was de Rochefort? Did he carry a message from the King of France to the imprisoned Charles I? Or did he come from Cromwell, assigned to murder Charles? Whose side was he on?

The old Tudor building that was once the inn is now a waxworks. Here visitors can see these grisly bits of history displayed there in wax. It is believed to be one of the oldest buildings in town.

Now jumping a few centuries, in 1964, while digging for a water pipe, work-men were confronted by a human skeleton. The idea was seized upon that this must be the remains of Louis de Rochefort, and it was decided to send the bones to France, where he could be given a Christian burial by his descendents. But no descendents were found in his home town of Rochefort and the skeleton was returned to Brading where it is now exhibited in the museum – where it is referred to as 'Lonely Louis'.

In the early 1970s, a transparent form of a tall, thin man was seen gliding along the balcony. And the appearance of Lonely Louis in the house was said to be so scary that the tenant in the house moved out 'in a great hurry'.

Andrew, writing in 1980, says that one of the best tests to see if a ghost is near is to confront it with an animal. Having done this here, he says that the dogs got 'extremely distressed' in the corner of the bedroom where the Frenchman was thought to have met his end.

The old Tudor building that was once an inn is now a waxworks. (courtesy of Ralph Edermaniger)

In February 2006, Southern Paranormal made an investigation with all the paraphernalia that every ghost-hunter seems to carry these days. A number of orbs were seen (orbs are balls of light said to be a precursor to the appearance of an actual ghost). The team was uneasy and had the feeling of being watched. There were reports of people's hair being stroked, and a small girl was sensed, as well as seen, on the upper stairs of the house. An angry man was also said to be walking around the house and being very cross at being disturbed. Footsteps and doors banging were heard, though there were no doors in that part of the building.

In other words, the building housing Brading the Experience, is in every way a haunted house, carried over the centuries. With real ghosts.

So watch it!

BRADING THE EXPERIENCE
BRADING, ISLE OF WIGHT
OPEN AT THE APPROPRIATE HOURS
TEL: 01983 407286

FIFTEEN

Kent

BRIDGE PLACE COUNTRY CLUB

The pitiful cries of a murdered baby

Things haven't changed much here since Andrew's *Our Haunted Kingdom*. The baby's cries still come from the chimney breast in a ground floor room. The ghost of the mother, a chambermaid – for she was also murdered – is still seen with a laundry basket in one of the bedrooms. According to Peter Malkin, still the owner of the Bridge Place Country Club, he sees the chambermaid with the laundry basket every month or two. He is very calm and matter-of-fact when he spoke to me. Of course he's heard the baby cry, but not recently. Which must be a comfort.

For the origins of this ghastly tale, we have to look back into the eighteenth century. In about 1780, the owner of the manor house, as it then was, was a man called Taylor. He had been carrying on an illicit affair with the chambermaid while his wife was in Scotland, recovering from a long illness. He had in fact fathered a baby with the chambermaid. Hearing that his wife was returning, he thought he had little option but to murder mother and child – and this he did.

One wonders where he hid the bodies. Could the baby have been shoved up the chimney – which was where the cries came from? The young mother under the floor of the bedroom where she now appears? Of course we don't know, but speculation is rife from many who've visited the house.

There is another story, and it comes from 1969 when a young French boy was staying in the haunted bedroom. What he saw was what he described as a 'Cavalier-type figure of a man.' When the same phantom appeared on the subsequent night, he asked for another room – a request that was willingly granted.

This attractive old building was constructed as a manor house in 1638. It was partly destroyed in the English Civil War (1642-1646 and 1648) and eventually converted into a popular country club complete with a large dance floor in the original wing. It still has its seventeenth-century oak stairway and carved stone busts. The present owner, Peter Malkin, bought the club in 1967 and, shortly after he had moved in, was astonished by its entrenched ghosts. They seldom bother him now. He is used to them. They are used to each other.

BRIDGE PLACE COUNTRY CLUB
BREWERY LANE, BRIDGE, CANTERBURY, KENT, CT4 5LF
TEL: 01227 830308
OPEN TO THE PUBLIC BY APPOINTMENT ONLY

DOVER CASTLE

Centuries of ghosts appearing today

In his 1999 *Haunted Kent Today*, Andrew gave a good coverage of the ever-recurring phantoms at Dover Castle. We've gone a little further in this chapter but given space for Andrew to comment from time to time. New parts of the castle have been opened up and surprises keep happening.

So when I asked Christine Pascall, one of the ghost-walk guides, what was new, she replied: 'Ghosts are not always sensational (though we do have our share of those). Sometimes they are as trivial (and as inexplicable) as the ghost who last week blew in a visitor's ear. A couple of weeks before that, a 'rough voice' sounded in one of the numerous tunnels. He said, (again quite inexplicably), 'Gawd for that I'm home.' A voice out of nowhere – in one of the country's most haunted places.

Dover Castle, which dates from the twelfth century, holds a number of ghosts, perhaps immersed in its ancient stone – some held there for over 900 years. The complex, physically, houses two chapels, the former secret underground command centre which played such an important role in the Second World War, and the medieval underground works which were adapted to protect Britain from Napoleon's anticipated invasion.

At approximately 6 o'clock on the evening of 19 June 1979, a male member of staff was locking up for the night, when he was startled by the appearance of an unexpected visitor. As bold as brass, in walked a seventeenth-century Cavalier pike man, wearing a Morion helmet. The guide had not fully recovered his equilibrium when the soldier calmly walked out through the walls of the guardroom.

Sometime in 1991, in one of the many underground tunnels, two American tourists effusively thanked their guide for the good show he had put on. But the guide had to point out that – effective as it was – the shrieking and moaning during the tour was not Dover Castle's doing. And there was nobody else in the tunnel besides themselves.

People-shaped images, strange sounds and peculiar smells sometimes proliferate in the castle. There's the often-seen figure in a blue cloak, the loud slamming of doors, sometimes where there are no longer doorways, and the strong, masculine smell of weed tobacco – where there were no smokers.

In 1991, according to Dover Castle records, the Thanet Psychic and Paranormal Research Unit teamed up with the Association for the Study of Anomalous Phenomena (ASAP) for the once only all-night paranormal investigation of Dover Castle. In *Haunted Kent Today*, Andrew considers the vigil one of great importance. He also cites other people who took part. They were led by Robin Laurence and the Thanet Research Unit. Others were a Meridian Television Team including Mike Debden, the presenter, sixteen members of the research group, Dr Chris Cherry of Kent University, and a fellow author and researcher, Dr Peter Moore. Eight specific locations were covered by the team members in a well-organised rota system, both in the keep and in the underground works.

The Dover Castle team compiled the following results by time:

> *10.23 p.m., sound of door slamming; 2.20 a.m., shadow seen moving down stairwell at end of lower passage, (at first, this was thought to be one of the other investigators but when they called him on the radio, it was discovered he was in another area); 3.15 a.m., sound of door slamming; 3.40 a.m., sound of door slamming (recorded on audio equipment in mid passageway of spur); 4.40 a.m., repeat of 3.40 a.m., (recorded again on audio); 5.15 a.m., several teams hear sounds of multiple doors slamming.*

Here, in deadpan prose, much of this may seem trivial, but this doesn't give the whole picture. Perhaps what the investigators might not have known was that the survey was recorded, not only in sound on their tape recorders, but also on film to be shown on a mini-documentary television programme. For as Andrew says, 'to see a pair of massive doors being shaken at 5.20 in the morning, as if by some invisible giant, was to many viewers, let alone the investigators, an incredible and undeniable example of proof of poltergeist phenomena.'

It's important to realize that much of Dover castle – those parts of Napoleonic origins and the Second World War rooms – were closed until the 1990s. It is therefore interesting that most of the very many sightings have taken place in the last seventeen or so years. We'll look at some of the most interesting.

A staff member (whom we shall call Tom) was locking up for the night, when he saw a figure at the end of the Mess Room, looking at the photograph of Winston Churchill. Tom described it as appearing very odd. The figure looked up from what he was studying and immediately took off down the RAF dormitory. Because it was so realistic, Tom thought it might be a member of the public. So he shouted at the apparition. He then searched the whole place and found nobody. He checked that no staff were working late. There were none. No alarms had been set off. Was it just a ghost he saw?

The next two incidents took place in the operating theatre. The guide, whom we shall call Charlie, was conducting a ghost tour. He saw a figure in uniform peering through a far door. Thinking he must be part of his group, he gathered them all around him and counted them. Everybody was there. No one was missing. So who was the figure in uniform?

The tunnels had a variety of uses during the Second World War; one tunnel was used as a morgue. During the war and in subsequent years, the complex was heavily guarded as part of the National Secrecy Act. No information was released until the late 1980s. It is therefore somewhat chilling to read that in the late 1970s, more than thirty years after the war, a team of builders working here reported seeing 'dead bodies lying everywhere.'

The next incident also concerns Tom, the man cited earlier, locking up for the night. It was some months later. As he was about to leave the Gallery, he described hearing a very loud screeching sound, one that sounded as though a table (or a heavy body?) was being dragged over the stone floor. Tom immediately checked the room to see where the sound was coming from. Nothing. As he was leaving the complex he made the same enquiries as before. No one had left the complex. No alarms had sounded.

Dover Castle from an old print. Ask about the ghost tours. (courtesy of English Heritage)

Dover Castle by night – simply breathtaking, but when the sun goes down, the little ghosties come out to play. (courtesy of English Heritage)

The Casemate was quite important during wartime operations and was the room used by Vice Admiral Bertrim Ramsay. The guide here, whom we shall call Judy, did what all her colleagues did. As she guided her flock through the various haunted tunnels, she put the light on in the next room, ahead of everybody. In this case, she switched on the light as usual. But this time, as soon as it was on, all the lights in the complex went out, one by one. Summoning the ghost, in her most commanding (and angry) voice, she called: 'OK come on turn them on please!' The lights came on again, one by one. There was nobody in the vicinity.

The most haunted room in Dover Castle is famous for the ghost of a naval officer, dressed in blue, who stalks the back of the room. Visitors are frequently asked if they have clearance to be in the room and can they show him their documentation. Many believe it to be part of the tour until a guide calmly tells that it's not, that they don't employ reenactors. In 1992, he reportedly walked down the casemate, through the barrier and through a member of the public, causing the victim to fall over. In October 2004, a guide was delivering his tour speech from this room when he heard clear footsteps come from behind and then felt something pass through him. The guide was reported to be as white as a sheet.

Back in the 1940s, the Royal Navy employed a cat as a ratter and mouser for the tunnel complex; the cat was called Dave. Sadly, Dave somehow got himself trapped in a crevice and died before anybody noticed. Ever afterwards, guides have come back from opening the tunnels up and reported hearing a cat in distress. At another time, a manager actually saw a cat and gave chase. The staff are convinced that such are the security arrangements, a real cat could not get through. So was it Dave?

Two incidents occurred in what was the Officers' New Barracks. The first involved a member of staff carrying out some repair work when she felt she was being watched. She looked up and saw a figure in a long black cloak. She saw the figure walk off to the left, towards a dead end that had been securely boarded up. The figure in the long black cloak has never been seen again.

The second incident is even stranger. A staff member parked her car one morning, ready for work when she looked up and in the top window saw a dark figure peering out. In the evening, returning to her car, she looked up, looking for the same window. It was only then that she realised that there was no top window: that whole section of the building had no first and second floor any more. The floors had been stripped out during the 1960s.

The 'Lady in Red' is probably the castle's most famous ghost. On several occasions, custodians have spotted a lady in red on the second floor – in the day and in the night. This has always been followed by thorough searches and nobody has been located – mortal or spirit. The Lady in Red has also been seen in the Gallery and by the west stairs. These sightings have usually been accompanied by the sound of sobbing. She is a tragic figure.

On a quite different sighting, one morning in 1990, a cleaner saw a man wearing a black brimmed hat and a purple cloak draped to the floor. His hair was dark and wavy and he had a moustache. The style was Cavalier, circa 1610-1630. She didn't try to converse with him, although he looked solid enough.

In summing up, the guides at Dover Castle insist that belief is a very personal thing. What you have read in these pages is an almost complete list of the supernatural goings-on at Dover Castle. Every type of occurrence has at some time been reported – from the hearing of odd sounds, sensing strange smells, receiving repetitive and one-off visions, interactive communicative run-ins, to sentient poltergeist activity. What you believe to be is a matter of personal belief and personal belief only. Whether they are spirits from another planet, trapped echoes of the past or hysteria and hallucination, is for you to speculate.

I'm sure Andrew would agree.

DOVER CASTLE
OPEN TO THE PUBLIC AT THE APPROPRIATE HOURS
GHOST TOURS ARE ON FRIDAYS AND SATURDAYS FROM THE
BEGINNING OF NOVEMBER TO THE END OF FEBRUARY
TEL: 01304 211067. EASY ACCESS FROM A2 AND M20

PLUCKLEY VILLAGE

Pluckley's faded glory

We met the old man soon after we had arrived in Pluckley. His long blonde locks fell to his shoulders; his face was weathered thanks to an outdoor life and creased with age. He knew his home village. He knew Pluckley well. 'I've been here forty two years,' he said, 'and never seen a ghostie yet.'

The old man no doubt spoke for many in Pluckley, the village that once lived by the title of the most haunted village in the country. But the traditional side of the argument is staunchly defended by the new landlord of the Black Horse, Kevin Savage, who grew up in the village. About three weeks before he took over the pub, he had this ghostly experience. I'll let him tell it in his own words:

> *It was about two o'clock in the morning and I couldn't sleep. My wife and I lay snug in our bed with the nineteen-month-old baby in his own little bed just near to my wife. I suddenly realised that a sort of mist, person-shaped, was hovering over the baby. At the same time I felt a nice, warming feeling, calming, saying; 'don't worry about a thing'. I must have taken my eye off our ghost for an instant – for a ghost is what it must have been – and when I looked again, it had gone. The whole episode couldn't have lasted more than a minute.'*

It is stories like that which keep Pluckley on the haunted lists. I was visiting the village with Daryl Burchmore, an official English Heritage guide on his day off. He had kindly offered to show me around. After an excellent pub lunch, we visited some of Andrew's original Pluckley hauntings, published in 1973.

From the Black Horse (known for its poltergeist), we drove to Station Road, where a man, his wife and a dog met their deaths and came back again as spectres. It was believed that it might have been suicide.

We moved on to the Dering Arms (which pulls an excellent pint). For years, an old woman was seen to appear and disappear in the window here. In the High Street, a phantom coach and horses was spotted from time to time galloping silently down the street, striking terror into the hearts of the villagers who saw the apparition. St Nicholas' church is known for two hauntings. A Lady in Red – more about her later -has been seen gliding amongst the tombstones, forever searching for her daughter. And for those brave enough to visit the vault of the wicked but beautiful Lady Dering, they may see her clasping a red rose to her breast. Is she asking for forgiveness? She had a bad press from all accounts, but nobody knows why.

Then there is Fright Corner, its name changed by a ghost-hunter or two from the innocent Frith Corner. Like everywhere in Pluckley there is, of course, a story to go with the place. The exploits of a certain highwayman had made him an outlaw. For years he had fought off everyone who had gone in search for him. At last at Fright Corner, he was a sword's length away from capture. Bravely the outlaw fought back to attack. This showed the tremendous power of the smugglers. In open defiance of the law, in 1829, about eighty smugglers openly displayed twelve carts of contraband through the middle of the town, past streets of cheering crowds.

Writing in 1980, Andrew devoted nearly a page in small type to the George Hotel ghosts. He mentions one unique ghost in the following account.

A Janet Wicks was sleeping in one of the hotel's three-bedded rooms with her fifteen-year-old daughter, Lisa. At 7.30 a.m. Lisa left to go to work. 'About an hour later', Janet said, 'I felt something like a cat jump on to the bed, but there was nothing to be seen. I lay down again and suddenly felt the vibration of the unseen "thing" jump on to the floor and felt the tremor as it landed on the boards. But there was nothing there.' Janet got up and looked around the room, under the beds, even in the cupboards, but there was nothing that could explain what was going on. It might have been forgotten altogether had Mrs Wicks not discussed the experience with her sister-in-law, who was also living in the hotel. Mrs Wicks told her that she had suffered from an identical encounter some four months earlier at about 12.44 a.m.

According to Andrew, a young child is often involved in such incidents where there is one in the house. In this case, a five-year-old boy was living on the premises. It seems that he, too, had felt the invisible 'cat' on his bed and on one occasion he had seen the animal, a second before it disappeared. 'It just wasn't there any more.' Some years ago when another young lad was staying at the George, reports had been made of a similar haunting.

Up to about nine months earlier there had been a resident cat which frequently slept in the affected bedroom, but, sadly, pussy disappeared and has never been seen since – at least in physical form.

Finally, another visitor claimed that the door to their bedroom – the one that houses the 'invisible' cat, suddenly opened on its own account, and then slammed it shut with such force the whole room shook.

Could it be a 'gentleman' – as Kipling called smugglers – coming back for his loot? Maybe he had a pet cat.

GEORGE HOTEL
11 HIGH STREET, LYDD, KENT, TN29 9AJ,
TEL: 01797 321710.
OPEN TO THE PUBLIC AT THE APPROPRIATE TIMES

The Black Horse, still the best place to find a ghost and a pint in Pluckley.

against crack troops. Then one of the troopers gave an almighty thrust with his sword: the blade passed right through the body of the highwayman and impaled him to the tree. His carcass was left there to rot. Now even the oak tree that held him is gone.

We drove on through other parts of Pluckley. 'There's Greystones with its monk-ghosts,' Daryl said, pointing to a rather square, white house near the centre of the village. Pluckley is quite spread out. In Dering Woods a colonel once hanged himself and there have been sightings of a man in uniform. There used to be a mill around these parts and a ghostly miller can sometimes be seen. He is reputed to have committed suicide over a lost love. Still another phantom, a seller of watercress, took an afternoon nap with her lit pipe still in her mouth, so the story goes. The pipe fell out onto her clothes and set them alight. She has been seen from time to time as a glowing ball of fire. The old Brickworks too have disappeared – a worker once fell to his death there and screams can still be heard from time to time. In 1920, a teacher in Dickie Bus Lane took his own life. But to my knowledge, no ghost has emerged to remember his life and death.

Back in 1973, when Andrew published *Our Haunted Kingdom*, he found some half dozen or so ghosts here (others seem to have found twice that number). But by the time of his 1999 *Haunted Kent Today*, Andrew was reduced to writing about only one or two Pluckley ghosts.

Andrew certainly put flesh on the bones of the stories I had discussed with Daryl. Andrew writes that back then in the 1970s there was a poltergeist at Elvey Park Farm, another in the Black Horse, and – the most interesting to us – the ghostly figure of a woman in red in the churchyard adjoining the tavern.

At the Black Horse, around eleven o'clock one night, an eighteen-year-old barmaid, Anne Barham, decided to take a short cut home via the graveyard and, being local and used to all the tales, had no fears at all of 'any old spectres'. The following is Anne's story as told to Andrew:

> *When only a few feet into the area, I noticed that a woman was obviously searching for something and intently looking at the tomb-stones near the church. At first I wasn't worried. But then I realised that the cemetery's night visitor was wearing red and I felt anyway, that it was a bit strange for anyone to be searching a cemetery at that time of night. As I moved nearer though, she moved through two of the upright stones and at that, I'm afraid, I ran back to the pub. John (the chief barman), gave me a brandy and arranged to take me home. I'd never drunk spirits before, but he assured me, I really needed it.*

That's Pluckley today. Not the most haunted village in the country perhaps – but haunted, nonetheless. And well worth a visit.

PLUCKLEY VILLAGE, KENT
OPEN TO GHOSTS AT ANY TIME

Fright Corner. They impaled an outlaw to a long ago oak tree here. You wouldn't believe it today – even the tree has gone.

GEORGE HOTEL

Welcome to the hotel with the smell of death

'It was a customs man,' Tim Cromptom, landlord of Lydd's George Hotel told me. He was murdered here and left undetected under the floor for six months. 'When it materialises – as it sometimes does – the smell is something dreadful. It's the smell of death. But you could literally walk through it, in and out,' he told me. The murder and violence would not have been this unusual in a hotel with a long history of smugglers. But leaving the corpse under the floorboards certainly was: 'Come on in' Tim laughs, 'and if you're unlucky, you may even catch a whiff yourself.'

In a cutting from the *Kentish Express* of 18 March 1999, the reporter Joanna Hernon, in full journalistic flow, begins her piece with 'Ghosts, smugglers, sex and violence litter the history of the George Hotel in Lydd High Street'. Well, she does have a point. This was a real smuggler's inn, which was accustomed to smugglers and their ways. As for sex and violence, there was probably a good portion of these. To many, these were the 'gentlemen.' Almost everyone stood to benefit. Kipling was right in his 'brandy for the parson, whisky for the clerk'. But the ghosts continue to haunt the hotel to this day.

The present inn was built during the reign of James I in 1620 and remained the George Inn until 1865, when it became a registered hotel. Today, it is owned by Tim Crompton, who has the most bizarre stories to tell. There is one phantom who glides through the bar and up the staircase where there (now) isn't one. There is another ghost who appears in the lounge that used to be a judges' parlour. Tim says there are often two ghosts there, one pleading, the other swearing with all the cussing known to man, at the pleader. Tim continues:

> *'room six is supposed to be haunted. The story goes that the old mayor's chamber was connected to this room and he used to entertain ladies there. The ghost could be connected to these illicit encounters. Or – perhaps more likely – this was the room where one of the smugglers hanged himself.'*

Early nineteenth-century maps show that the sea was closer than it is now, and lapped against the town's borders. In March 1721, two of the infamous Mayfield gang, Jacob Walter, and Thomas Bigg, were captured as they came ashore from a French vessel near Dungeness lighthouse. They were taken in chains to the George and locked in a room, guarded by six armed blockade officers.

But the smugglers had some well-armed friends. Suddenly, nine burst in and rushed the guards. A local man, Stanton Blacklocks, was an eye-witness. He said; 'there were nine mounted men, with pistols, swords, and forks, who came up to the house.' They dismounted from their horses and ran upstairs, shooting all the way. They wounded three officers but managed to rescue Walter and Bigg.' If they had not succeeded there were apparently up to a hundred more smugglers waiting for the command

THEATRE ROYAL

'The most haunted theatre in Britain'

The most haunted theatre in the country – Margate's Theatre Royal – is also the UK's second-oldest (second to London's Old Vic). In *Haunted Kent Today*, Andrew has updated several of his earlier books and tells us why we should take this theatre's output of ghosts so seriously. Strange things keep on happening at the Theatre Royal and new hauntings seem to be taking place all the time. 'Ghosts here,' as the theatre's manager, Michael Wheatley-Ward, told me are 'an on-going thing.' Clock hands move unbidden, voices are heard, screams seem to come out of nowhere.

The building first opened as a theatre in 1787, but to the end of the eighteenth and halfway through the nineteenth century, the space had many uses and a number of managers. But in 1855, there began what the Theatre Royal likes to call its Thorne Dynasty. Richard Thorne, a man from a theatrical family, took over as manager and the theatre blossomed.

Sarah Thorne – now probably the theatre's favourite ghost – succeeded her father in the flesh in the early 1860s. She had been on the stage since the age of eighteen but had spent a number of years in Ireland where she had two illegitimate children. They were good years for the theatre under Sarah, and she acted as well as managed. Her stewardship saw the building of the new auditorium in 1874 and didn't come to an end until she died in 1899.

The building continued its multi-functional role. It was reopened as a theatre in 1930 but became a venue for all-in wrestling some years later. Throughout the twentieth century, the building suffered a number of vicissitudes and was in turn a cinema, a theatre and a bingo hall.

Such treatment of her famous boards was enough to bring the ghost of Sarah Thorne back from the blackness and into her theatre. The first sightings of her as a ghost were in 1918 but it wasn't until later that she caused such a commotion that the officers of the law had to be summoned. The exact date isn't recorded but after one appearance, her wraith was so frightening that some of her witnesses brought in a policeman. But this was no job for a bobby. How can a cop arrest a will-o'-the-wisp?

The journalist Fred Archer began writing about the theatre's ghostly side after the First World War. In describing Margate's Theatre Royal, Archer writes that 'there is a trapdoor (from the theatre) to what was a smugglers' cave.' He claims that the theatre probably boasts more diverse psychic happening than any theatre in the world. Archer describes an 'orange-coloured ball of light,' and a scream 'which starts backstage and seems to travel across the stage which finally exits through the stage door.' He also describes the appearance of a ghost in one of the boxes whose exploits have become a favourite story of Margate's Theatre Royal.

This is a story about this man-in-the-box. In the early 1900s, an actor from the theatrical company was fired. We don't know why but the next evening he bought himself one of the highest boxes – with a deadly purpose. During the performance, he hurled himself to death into the orchestra pit. From then onwards, this phantom occupies the box and has been seen so often that the management had to withdraw that box from sale, leaving it permanently curtained off. Today the top box is still closed – for health and safety reasons. Anyway, it would be too high for modern audiences. (They are the official reasons but we ghost-hunters know a thing or two, don't we?)

In *Haunted Kent Today*, Andrew wants us to appreciate the importance of this haunted theatre among those that know about these things. Among the eminent people who took a lot of interest in the theatre and spent a great deal of time there are: Dr ARG Owen of Cambridge; members of the Association for the Scientific Study of Anomalous Phenomena (ASSAP); Ena Twigg, one of the country's most respected mediums; and of course the theatrical world's Macqueen Pope. Ms Pope did see a ghost near the orchestra pit and assumed it to be the actor who had killed himself (as described above).

Members of the respected Ghost Club and others from local research groups held all-night-vigils in the building but nothing significant appeared. (As Andrew knew to his cost, if you go looking for a ghost, you won't find one.)

Perhaps the most-often-seen ghost – if you can call it a ghost – has appeared to many people as an orb, a floating globe of light. It is often believed this is the first stage of the appearance of an apparition. A popular ghost among many people is the man in a pork-pie hat who, according to Michael Wheatley-Ward, 'appeared just last week.' There is a tunnel – another tunnel – from the theatre to the adjacent pub called Everybody's Inn, and a ghost has recently been seen in the pub. 'Obviously an actor', the theatre manager told me. 'He was kitted out as a Cavalier'. Could he, perhaps, be the ghost with no name – the actor who crashed to his death from the box into the orchestra pit? I wonder will we ever know?

Finally, here is a recent story from an Australian visitor to the theatre. He and his friend were sitting in row D in the front stalls. Every now and again, he noticed his friend turn around sharply several times during the performance. After the show, he asked his Australian friend the reason. 'Somebody – some thing – kept tapping me on the shoulder', he said. 'When I turned round, the seats behind me were empty, there was nobody within reach.' He was quite unnerved by the experience.

I wonder how satisfied the Aussie would be with Mr Wheatley-Ward's parting shot to me. 'I want you to know', he said, 'our staff respect our ghosts. They are all quite friendly spirits.' And if anyone would know, it's him. After all, the present manager has been in the post for the second longest time, second only to Sarah Thorne.

THEATRE ROYAL
ADDINGTON STREET, MARGATE, KENT, CT9 1PW.
TEL: 01843 293397
OPEN TO THE PUBLIC DURING NORMAL HOURS

SIXTEEN

Lancashire

SMITHILLS HALL

The bloody footprint and other ghostly surprises

At the entrance to the withdrawing room of Smithills Hall Historic House, pro-tected by a metal shutter, is a mysterious mark, in the shape of a footprint on the flagstone. It was the heart-felt protest of a Protestant martyr, the preacher George Marsh, and took place during his interrogation for heresy. At one point in the long-winded proceedings, the exasperated prisoner ran from the room, raced down the stairs and stamped his foot hard upon the stone floor, crying as he did so: 'If I am true to my faith, God shall leave his mark.' Described as 'looking up to heaven,' he appealed to God for the justness of his cause and prayed that there might in that place remain a constant memorial to the wickedness and injustice of his enemies. But on 24 April 1555 – refusing to recant – George Marsh was burnt at the stake.

Andrew, writing in 1973, adds a sentence or two to the Marsh story. Apparently, George had made his escape and would have managed to travel abroad, except for one thing. They took his mother hostage. At that, what could he say? What could he do? He returned to face the music.

There is a story (which must have predated 1730) of how the footprint stone was once dug up and tossed into the nearby stream because of its unpleasant smell and eerie associations. But while the stone was so ignobly treated, the Hall was visited by the seven plagues of Egypt. When the stone was returned to its rightful place, there were no more disturbances.

According to tradition, the footprints are supposed to run blood every year on 24 April, the anniversary of Marsh's execution.

George Marsh has not been forgotten today, as there have been recent sightings of his ghost, dressed as a monk, in the chapel. Other sightings – the Hall attracts a lot of free spirits – have been a mother and child fighting and then the child crying. The same sounds have been heard by a member of staff around locking-up time in the museum.

In 1855, the renowned American author, Nathaniel Hawthorne, came to visit Smithills Hall, specifically to see the footprint. He made this comment: 'The Bloody

Footstep seemed fresh, as if it had been that very night imprinted anew, and the crime made all over again, with fresh guilt upon somebody.'

There now follows a legend from the undated past of bloody footsteps, more dreadful (and less believable) than the last. A certain lord, Sir Forester, living at Smithills, got it into his head that he could live forever if he performed a human sacrifice once every thirty years.

He had living with him a beautiful young kinswoman, an orphan, for whom he was responsible. Luring the poor girl into a nearby wood, the aged lord killed her swiftly with a knife and buried her body on the spot. But Nature, it seems, cries out for justice, and every footstep the ancient lord took left a bloody imprint. The trail of blood led from the site of the murder, through the woods, up the steps and even into the aged lord's bedroom.

Half crazed at the sight of the bloody trail he fled from the Hall, but the blood-red footsteps followed wherever he chose to go, even into the King's court. He returned to Smithills Hall where the servants were aghast at the bloody footsteps and struck with horror. The old lord, half crazed, fled his home and was never heard of again in the flesh. It is said that there is a ghost whose bloody footsteps drop blood. It would seem to be the old lord himself, but nobody knows for sure.

The Hall organises Ghost Trail evenings during which they discuss a number of Smithills Hall ghosts. The first takes place in the desolate series of upper rooms which once accommodated the female servants. There is a steep staircase and it is from the top here that a servant girl, Tilley Houghton, threw herself down to her death.

It was the old, old story, which took place about a hundred years ago. A local lad got Tilley pregnant, but when she told the father, he wanted nothing to do with Tilley or her child. Victorian social codes gave little hope: as soon as her employers found out, she would have been sanctimoniously dismissed without a reference. Carrying the stigma of bearing a child out of wedlock, she would have found most avenues of employment closed to her. Her only hope would probably have been the dreaded workhouse. But had she survived the fall down the stairs, she would have been charged with the serious crime of attempted suicide.

As it happened, the fall broke her neck and she must have died instantly. But the story doesn't end there. To this day, people still hear the forlorn sounds of a woman sobbing and the frantic footsteps coming from the unoccupied servants' bedrooms. Some claim – and this has not been verified – that they see a despairing young woman's face impressed upon the flagstones just below the door.

As the ghost tour approached the Great Hall, the guide asked us to use our imagination. Go back 600 years, she said, when the Great Hall had no heating, was virtually without light and holes which later inhabitants would fill in with glass and call them windows. In the flickering winter gloom, who wouldn't see all manner of ghosts? Add to this, the sudden fall in temperature that seems to occur whenever spirits are abroad. In the late evening heavy pacing footsteps have often been heard echoing across the ancient stones of the empty hall. On rare occasions, you can hear the muffled sound of two voices – one a man's, the other a woman's. They are locked in heated discussion.

The several psychic mediums who have visited Smithills Hall have all detected the presence of an imposing male figure in fifteenth-century attire, and a woman who appears to be beseeching him in a state of great distress.

The guide now suggests something entirely implausible. 'We know,' she says, 'that during the Wars of the Roses the last Lord Radcliffe to own Smithills Hall fought and died in the battle of St Albans, leaving behind him no male heir to inherit the estate. It is certainly possible that his wife, sensible of the danger, would have tried in vain to dissuade him going off to fight. Could the mysterious voices in the Great Hall then be those of Lord Radcliffe and his wife, endlessly rehearsing the same futile discussion, before he rides to join the Lancastrian forces at St Albans to meet his fate?' Well, it makes a good story.

The tour continues to room number four. The first ghost here looks very much as if it could be a cat. Going up the stairs to the Solar Room, many visitors have mentioned something brushing gently against their legs, shoulder, or back. Could it be – as our imaginative guide suggests – the Ainsworth cat which fell to its death from an upper window in 1872. Well, it makes another good storey.

The next ghost, still in the Solar Room, has been the indistinct figure of a woman, dressed all in black. In the 1950s, during some renovation work on the Hall, some human bones were found.

It is interesting to note an extraordinary reaction one visitor had to the Smithills Hall ghost tour. The guide had just begun her Withdrawing Room spiel. This is how it was reported:

Our guide had just paused to discuss some of the figures carved on the Tudor panelling when one of the women in the group appeared to take a strange turn. First she complained of being suddenly cold. Then she fell silent and her face grew ghastly pale. Her lips were moving as if in silent prayer, and her eyes grew dark and concentrated as she gazed upon the wooden countenance of Cecily Barton. Shocked by the sudden change, our guide asked her if something was wrong, if she felt unwell. But the woman did not respond; her attention was fixed entirely on the carved portrait. As if in a trance, she drifted forward and brought her hand up toward the panelling. For a moment she stood caressing the wooden relief, her lips softly parted with a sort of heady childish wonder.

Unsure of what else to do, the guide stepped forward and put his hand on the woman's shoulder. He later described how it was, a terrifying icy sensation comparable to nothing he had ever felt before or since. He took the transfixed woman's body into his own outstretched arms. Somehow, his intervention seemed to break the spell that held the woman enthralled, and she fainted backwards into his arms. It took several moments before she regained consciousness, and even after fully recovering she could recall very little of what had occurred.

Rather embarrassed, she insisted that she did not know what had come over her. When pressed, all she would say was: 'When I saw that woman's face, it was like the years fell away and I was staring into a mirror.' And with that, she left, leaving no hope of quizzing her further.

The next contact with a ghost, or rather, ghosts, took place on a dull, miserable, late December day, not at all the kind of weather you would expect to find groups of children happily playing outside. It was the sound of laughter, shrieks of delight, but when a staff member looked outside, there was nothing to be seen. And this happened several times.

Another mysterious sound has been galloping horses, the sound of whinnying and the crack of the whip. In the middle of the night, the noise was enough to wake people sleeping in the Hall. In an effort to find who these phantom horsemen could have been in life, those at the Hall looked back to the English Civil War in the mid-seventeenth century.

As most of the town of Bolton was on the side of Parliament, they put up a fierce resistance when the Royalists tried to pass through the town. After a siege lasting several days, the Royalists entered the town and put more than half the population, including women and children, to the sword. Those trying to escape on horseback raced past Smithills Hall, in all likelihood hotly pursued by the Parliamentarians.

The story earns more credence when we consider what took place when the Mayor of Bolton visited Smithills Hall recently. He claimed to have seen two men in Royalist uniform ambling across the lawn from the withdrawing room window. There was no costumed event planned for that day. So who were the two mysterious figures, phantoms of his imagination or more restless ghosts from Bolton's bloody past?

The Green Chamber is the Hall's most haunted room. It was in this room that George Marsh was held and interrogated. Imagine him here pondering on the horrors and the suffering about to be his. He is ready to defend his version of the Bible, a belief so strong that he is quite ready to die for it, even to endure the agonies of being burnt at the stake.

The first written report of the supernatural in the Green Chamber dates from 1732 and comes from the diary of a man who boarded here. The little sleep he managed to get was disturbed by a voice in prayer and then by a ghostly apparition of a man who came before his bed, and stood staring down with an expression of great intensity towards him. The gentleman noted in his diary that he had been paid a visit by George Marsh – the first of many encounters.

On a ghost evening in 2006, George Marsh was caught on camera and the photograph is on display in Smithills Hall. In April 2007, George was asked a question, and a disembodied voice was heard to respond to the question.

In the chapel, there have been several sightings of a figure kneeling in prayer before one of the pews, at the far end or the building. When approached, he simply disappears.

In the Drawing Room named after a Colonel Ainsworth, the figure of the great man has been seen and often the aroma of a good cigar fills the air. Following these appearances, it is not uncommon to find that glasses have been found turned over during the night.

In the Ainsworth Dining Room, which is now the shop, one last ghost has been seen, this time in a large mirror. The guide turned round to see who the reflection was – but of course there was no one there. The ghost existed only in the mirror.

This has more or less followed the journey taken by the Smithills' guides. Like all such ghostly regions, it is often difficult to distinguish between ghost and reality. What you believe, only you can say. Those are the last words from Smithills Hall.

SMITHILLS HALL
SMITHILLS DEAN ROAD, BOLTON,
BL1 7MP, LANCASTER,
TEL: 01204 332377
OPEN TO THE PUBLIC AT THE APPROPRIATE TIMES

SAMLESBURY HALL

The ghost who pinches pretty bottoms

Samlesbury Hall in Lancashire has ghosts coming out of the woodwork, most of them the result of suffering in this grand old fourteenth-century manor house. And I hear there has been recent haunting in 2006. But before we can deal with the ghosts, a short history lesson is necessary.

The present structure is by no means the first house on this site and a very early building suffered from a raid in Lancashire by Robert the Bruce in July 1322. In his raid of destruction he attacked Samlesbury Hall and 'burned the old stone half'.

Extensive restructuring took place in the sixteenth century by the Southworth family. Sir Thomas Southworth inherited the family lands in Samlesbury in 1517 and he is best remembered for his rebuilding of large parts of Samlesbury Hall, much of which exists today.

It was, however, a later descendent of the family, Sir John Southworth, who caused the family most pain. From all accounts, Sir John was a peaceful sort of man. He was knighted in Scotland and was High Sheriff of Lancashire in 1561. But Sir John was a Catholic and here is where his trouble lay: all his life he was persecuted for his affiliation with 'the old religion'.

He had priest holes made in the fabric of the building, and at least one of the family was murdered by the Queen's men. It was in the 1550s and the priest, another John Southworth, was administering to the family. Somebody gave the alarm that armed men were coming and John was rushed into one of the mansion's priest holes. But alas, somebody must have tipped off the military, for they went straight to where the poor man was hiding. There was the sound of swords being drawn, and a scream. Blood gushed forth. In photographs, this blood – which you can see in the Priest's Room today – still appears blood red. Generations of servants have scrubbed that stain, but it won't budge. And the ghost of the Southworth priest still haunts this room; guests have reported feeling dizzy there.

Another ghost is that of Joseph Harrison, who owned the Hall in the 1870s. He committed suicide (why is not known) in the Minstrel Gallery. He is the playful ghost with a penchant for young blondes and has been known on occasion to pull the locks of the good looking ones and even to pinch their pretty bottoms!

But perhaps the most famous of Samlesbury Hall's ghosts is known as the White Lady. Lady Dorathea (or Dorothy), a supposedly good Catholic girl, made the mistake of falling for a young Protestant man by the name of de Houghton. Her father got wind of her liaison and told his daughter never to see her lover again – the father would not have a Protestant in his house. He warned his daughter that if she continued these trysts, she would be banished to a nunnery – there to spend the rest of her days away from men.

A touch of the Tudors adds atmosphere.

Reported to be one of the most haunted places in the country. (courtesy of Salmesbury Hall)

But true love, they say, will not be forsworn and the warning only strengthened her ardour and made her determined to see her Protestant love. So on a bright, moonlit night they met in the Hall's grounds, rushing into each other's arms. But as they were embracing and giving to each other forbidden kisses, Dorathea's two brothers appeared as if from nowhere. Young de Houghton was cruelly murdered in front of Dorathea. She was immediately banished to a nunnery in France. It was said that from that moment on, she never ate or slept again and died of a broken heart. Her ghost regularly appears in the Hall's grounds and stops at the place where her lover was believed to be buried, near the yew and chestnut trees.

There have been a number of sightings of the White Lady. Here is a sample: she has stopped buses on the nearby road and then disappeared; she has done the same with motorists, flagged down a taxi, got in, and disappeared during the journey; another tale is that a police car hit a lady in white, but when the constable got out to look there was no body and no bump on the front of the car. It has also been reported that she has sat comfortably in the back seat of cars. When sighted, she simply does her usual disappearing trick. She once appeared before two soldiers who were stationed near the Hall. When she materialized in front of them, one soldier was so frightened he suffered a seizure from which he never recovered.

For some time, Samlesbury Hall has organized ghost nights, run by two professional ghost-hunters. One of the two, Gary Johnson, has summarized the ghosts he has discovered; he believes that the Hall is one of the most haunted places in the country. Unusually, there have been physical contacts such as pulling and stroking of hair, the faint touch of unsourced breathing on you, and pushing. There have been electrical anomalies, and whistling. A photograph, taken by a visitor, when processed, showed 'a Tudor gentleman' in all his glory, 'with full beard and moustache.'

That photographer was lucky. In Gary's experience, the ghosts can have a debilitating effect on camera equipment. Gary has been known to go through as many as sixteen camera batteries, the power in all of them drained within seconds.

Other ghostly encounters have included raucous shouting and fighting and the wild behaviour of poltergeists. There have been the sounds of the smashing of crockery but when checked, nothing had been broken. Doors have been slammed and conversation heard when there was nobody else at home.

In Andrew's 1977 *Phantom Ladies*, he challenges the veracity of the story of Lady Southworth, the White Lady. He quotes the usual story of the White Lady and the murder of her lover, but then says that the 'family pedigree knows nothing of her existence.'

But adding to the mystery, Andrew says that a few years before his book was published, workmen fitting additional drainage revealed the major part of a man's skeleton lying against the foundation wall. Could this – as we speculated earlier in this entry – be the remains of de Houghton, Lady Dorothy's Protestant lover, murdered within the grounds of the Hall? It is within several feet of the spot where the White Lady has been seen gliding by.

SAMLESBURY HALL
PRESTON NEW ROAD, PRESTON, LANCASHIRE,
TEL: 01254 812229
OPEN TO THE PUBLIC SUNDAY TO FRIDAY 11 A.M. TO 4.30 P.M.

SEVENTEEN

Leicestershire

GRACE DIEU PRIORY

A host of ghosts

Thanks to the work of the Friends of Grace Dieu Priory Trust, a number of ghosts have been found occurring in or near the lovely ruins of the priory in Shepshed, Leicestershire. Grace Dieu Priory was founded by Rosia de Verdon as an Augustinian religious house for nuns in the mid-thirteenth century. This was dissolved in 1538. It was typical of the majority of nunneries established in England after the Norman Conquest, in that it was a priory rather than an abbey and its founder was of lesser rank. After the Dissolution it was used as a house but by 1730 the buildings were in ruins. In the nineteenth century this was taken up as a romantic ruin by William Wordsworth and other poets.

The first ghostly sighting occurred over eighty years ago and concerns six ghosts seen by Hetty Wilson in September 1926. Eleven-year-old Hetty had accompanied her family to Coalville, where her father had been selling horses. On their way home, passing the priory, the horse drawing their Landau stopped dead in its tracks and stood there quivering. The family all looked round to see what had caused such a sudden stop.

To their astonishment, they saw six figures coming out of the copse on the side of the road. Hetty remembers her father shouting 'Good God, ghosts!' Then, as they came nearer, chillingly, the young girl saw that the apparitions had no faces, hands or feet. In terror, she buried her head in her hands. When she forced herself to look again, the white-robed ghosts had crossed the road and were heading up towards the ruin. This was reported in the *Leicester Mercury* on 1 August 1995.

Charlie Gough had been a worker on the Grace Dieu Estate for some forty years and in 1948, just after the Second World War, he told his story, which spread like wildfire through the local communities. One night, after he had finished a normal working day on the estate, he encountered the spectral form of a nun. The old man remembered her dressed entirely in white and wearing a wide-brimmed hat. His story was reported in the *Leicester Mercury*, on 10 January 1964.

A passenger on the old Charnwood Forest Railway made one particularly frightening sighting. She remembered sitting in a carriage on a journey from Whitwick to Loughborough, when she and her two friends became aware of feeling intense cold as the train slowed for the Grace Dieu station near the ruins.

As the train passed the ruins, the passengers suddenly became aware of a white face peering into the dimly lit interior of the carriage, from the darkness outside. One of her friends got up and approached the window but the face had disappeared without a trace. When the train stopped at the station, they all looked out of the window, but there was no one outside the carriage or waiting on the platform.

Perhaps the most celebrated sighting of all occurred in 1954, when the driver of a bus travelling from Thringstone to Shepshed pulled up at the lonely bus shelter opposite the ruins to pick up a woman dressed all in white. The bus driver opened the doors of the bus but when he did so there was no one there. Both driver and conductor got out to look, astonished by the fact that the woman in white had simply vanished. The bus driver told the story to a number of people, including David Callaghan of Ellistown, who published it.

The story is now a puzzling piece of folklore and has been used as a basis for a number of newspaper articles. One such feature, published in the *Coalville Mail* in July 1996, attracted the attention of a very special bus passenger – Mrs Mary Bates of Coalville, then aged ninety-nine. She had been a bus passenger on that long-ago journey, and had actually seen the woman in white who disappeared.

The ghosts of Grace Dieu; from real ghosts to ghostly orbs. (courtesy of the Friends of Grace Dieu)

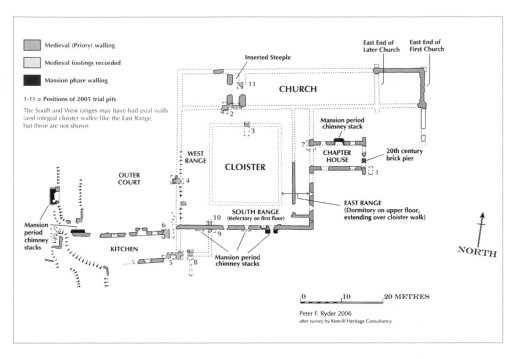

Grace Dieu Priory ground plan. (courtesy of the Friends of Grace Dieu)

In October 1997 a council worker was preparing the land around the ancient ruins for a Halloween ghost walk when he came face-to-face with a real ghost. It was none other than the legendary ghost of the Lady in White and it sent the man running away in terror.

Allen Scott-Davies, heritage manager for North-West Leicestershire District Council, was immediately sympathetic and said that it must have been a frightening experience. He said that it had just begun to get dark and that they were starting to pack up for the day, at that moment, the terror-stricken council man came running towards them, saying he'd seen a ghost.

Martin Redfern, an employee for the North-West Leicestershire District Council, added another voice. He was not normally afraid of anything, he said, but this experience was the exception: he was terrified. He had just been strimming grass along the side of the priory walls when he looked up and saw this lady in white standing next to him, watching him. Suddenly, he felt a strong push in the middle of his back: the strimmer hit the ground and he fell to his knees. When he looked around, the apparition had disappeared completely and he is adamant he did not slip accidentally. Mr Scott-Davies said that Martin had been as white as a sheet and genuinely scared. The poor lad had shaken for over an hour and said he refused to work there ever again.

On another occasion, Martin and Mr Scott Davies were clearing rubbish out of the Grace Dieu brook. Martin glanced up and saw the figure of a nun on a nearby bank; he mentioned this to Mr Scott-Davies but by the time he had looked around, the phantom had faded into obscurity.

Alan Scott-Davies regularly holds ghost walks around the priory on behalf of the North West Leicestershire District Council and has met several people who claim to have seen the ghost of the White Lady.

He explained that the priory was built around 1212 or 1213 and it was about 1530 when Agnes Litherland came to the priory as prioress. She was still in office when Henry VIII sent two people to assess the closing of the priory as part of his programme of closures. For some reason, Grace Dieu earned a reprieve. A couple of years later, however, word got out that one of the nuns was pregnant. Not only that; it was discovered that two of the nuns had been rather free with their favours, one, Agnes Litherland, with a local landowner. This was just the excuse Henry needed: Agnes and her lover were walled up with only eye slits in the bricks, and left to starve.

Back to the present. Alan Scott-Davies claimed that along with others, he had seen a figure dressed in black standing on the other side of the road from the priory. He hadn't been able to find out much about the ghost but maybe, just maybe, he was the nun's lover trying to find his love.

Back in 1977, when Andrew's *Phantom Ladies* was published we find two of his ghosts. One ghost is Roesia de Verdon, the founder of Grace Dieu Priory. The other is as modern as the motor car – though this one creates a mystery. He is supposed to have been the unfortunate victim of a car crash. Yet Andrew notes that there is no record of a fatal car crash near the site.

Andrew's description of the ghost of Roesia de Verdon is that she is 'old and bent' and that she has 'what looks like some kind of bag in her left hand'. There have been other sightings – she is 'in white from head to foot including her conical hat.' Yet another says that several motorists have seen her shuffling along some 50ft from the bus stop and one or two cars have stopped to offer her a lift – only to find that as soon as they get out of the car or open the door, the figure has vanished.

GRACE DIEU PRIORY
SHEPSHED, LEICESTERSHIRE.
TEL: 01530 454603
OPEN TO THE PUBLIC AT APPROPRIATE HOURS

EIGHTEEN

London

THE RELUCTANT GHOSTS AT THE ALBERT HALL

Monday 29 April 1996 was the night when Andrew really hit the headlines, and the world's press fell over each other to get a picture and an interview. It was ghost-hunting on a large scale and the next day's newspapers ran it as a major story.

For some time, there had been unexplained noises and sightings within the giant Albert Hall. As early as 1989, Rivers Howgill, then a night manager, saw two young women dressed in Victorian clothes in one of the corridors near the kitchens. 'I heard giggling and female talk', he said, 'so I went into the corridor where I saw the back view of these two women heading toward the kitchen. I went up to them and said 'Excuse me but you can't go in there, it's out of bounds.' They just faded into the blackness.' Were they, perhaps, ladies of the Victorian demi-monde? Years before the present hall was built in the nineteenth century, Gore House stood on the site and the Count O'Orsay ran a brothel in the basement.

The Albert Hall.

The area around the organ was said to be haunted by a stooped old man wearing a skull cap who berated workmen whenever repairs were carried out on the instrument. The apparition was thought to be that of Henry Willis, the organ's designer and the father of British organ building. For years there had been reports by the staff of 'feelings of unease' when patrolling the building in the depths of the night. And was it a spook or just a breakdown that caused the repeated failure of the basement alarm system?

The beginning of the 1996 Proms was just about upon them and it was just felt that something had to be done. Work was also due to start on installing new offices and previous sightings had often occurred during building work. Ian Blackburn, the Hall's director of building development, said that since the first sightings in the 1930s work-men and hall staff had often reported 'feelings of unease', strange noises or a sudden drop in temperature. 'When people keep saying the same things to you, you have to listen and take notice and try to get to the bottom of it', Mr Blackburn said. 'If there is going to be another sighting, it seems likely to be very soon.' Someone raised the subject of an exorcism. Would they pursue this in the event that evidence of ghosts was found? The answer was no. There were to be no dealings with exorcists.

The Albert Hall management contacted public relations consultant, Mark Borkowski, and asked him to find the best, most reliable ghost-hunter to come to their urgent aid. Andrew was plucked from the quiet of his eighteenth century Sussex cottage to the full glare of the world's scribblers and lensmen.

Andrew arrived with a full kit of ghost-detecting equipment, common now, but rare then. It included a night scope, anti-static pistol, high-frequency recording unit, digital thermometer, electricity detector and assorted cameras. He also brought with him a large quantity of common sense and a good sense of humour. And to accompany him, what seemed like much of the world's press.

Andrew's twelve-hour vigil became a scrimmage of journalists and of photographers zooming in for close-ups. 'Look this way, Andrew – get in a better light.' 'Hold up your equipment again, that's the way.' 'Can you try to look a bit more ghostly?' But for all his efforts, things ended as Andrew expected: 'look for a ghost and it will never appear'.

I asked the Albert Hall's archivist, Jacky Cowdrey, if there had been any recent sightings for this casebook. The answer was yes but nothing terribly significant. Staff on night duty have seen a floor-to-ceiling shimmering ball with black dots in the ladies' loo. There is sometimes what she could only call a feeling in the air, a sort of spooky something so much so that security officers have been known to be too scared to go up to the Gallery on their own at night. Do I hear someone say 'Bring back Andrew'?

THE ALBERT HALL
KENSINGTON GORE, LONDON, SW7.
BOX OFFICE: 02075 898212
OPEN TO THE PUBLIC AT THE APPROPRIATE HOURS.

BRUCE CASTLE MUSEUM

Some 150 ghostly revellers and not a sound to be heard

There are a number of ghostly things going on at the Bruce Castle Museum but perhaps the strangest are the references to garden parties in the early 1970s of a large gatherings of ghosts in the grounds. There is more than one report about this but the picture painted by a local paper, the now defunct *Weekly Herald*, is the most detailed. The paper claims that:

100 and possibly 150 ghosts were under the trees. The women were dressed in crinoline gowns, wore powdered wigs, and beauty patches. The men were in knee breeches, stockings, buckled shoes, and wore flowered coats.

Servants, dressed all in black, were circulating among the guests, and bowing as they served food and drinks. Some were playing croquet on the lawns, and there was a stage similar to that of a Greek theatre, where a play was in progress.

Everyone appeared to be enjoying themselves and faint music seemed to come from a small orchestra. The host was a parson, who was dressed in black and wore a white clerical collar.

The paper quotes a local Tottenham man who apparently spent an all-night vigil there with his wife. He told the reporter: 'we saw the ghosts melt into the walls of the castle like magic while we were making our rounds.'

It is interesting that this wild tale mentions a small orchestra playing audible music, as other sources state that there were no sounds from the revellers. And Andrew (see later) agrees.

The Bruce Castle Museum occupies one of what must be a diminishing number of Tudor buildings left in London. The former sixteenth- and seventeenth-century manor house for Tottenham became a school in 1827, run by Sir Roland Hill's family. After continued private occupancy for some 500 years, it was bought by the local council in 1906.

Since about 1858, there have been numerous reports of ghostly goings-on there. The most noted ghost appears to be Lady Constantia Lucy, the first wife of the second Lord Coleraine. He had grown to dislike her and had her confined in an upper room just below the clock tower. Driven insane by the constant ticking, she threw herself and her baby off a high balcony. Both perished. It was 2 November 1680 and every year on that date, it is believed her spirit returns and her despairing cries can be heard, carried on the wind.

The museum has a document detailing more than two dozen ghostly manifestations between the years 1957 to 1982. There are reports of poltergeist activity, phantom footsteps in empty rooms, pet dogs refusing to go to certain parts of the building, doors slamming when the air is still, 'terrible loud noises, like slates being smashed' and great sobbing coming from an empty women's lavatory. Many of these 'happenings' were reported to the local constabulary and are now recorded in police files. All such good evidence, I imagine, helped to earn the museum its place as the tenth most haunted building in London.

Andrew, in *Our Haunted Kingdom*, gives yet another account of the ghostly revellers in July 1971. A couple reported to him that on their walk, they saw 'a large number of people in eighteenth-century costume, apparently enjoying a festive occasion. But he emphasises, what we have already noted – 'despite the couple of dozen people present and the obvious frivolity, there was no sound and the figures seemed to glide rather than walk.'

A few days later, another couple were determined to find out the truth. They spent the night in the locality. They 'saw a dozen apparitions, all in olden days dress… when approached… the crowd just melted into the walls.'

Make a date in your diary. Bruce Castle claims an anniversary ghost visits them on 3 November each year.

BRUCE CASTLE MUSEUM
LORDSHIP LANE, TOTTENHAM, LONDON
OPEN TO THE PUBLIC AT THE APPROPRIATE TIMES

CROWN AND HORSESHOES

Their dog can 'see' a ghost even if you can't

There is something very uncanny about your average dog. They give you a signal. In talking to publicans, it always comes to the same thing. If their dog's hair rises up, they suspect a haunting. And properly speaking, so do you. You may not even hear anything or see anything different, but wherever you suspect the ghost to be, your dog simply won't go there. A dog is a kind of guardian between the natural and the psychic realm. At least, that's what they tell me.

This is precisely the 2007 ongoing experience of Mark and Lisa Chapman, the present licensees of the Crown and Horseshoes in Enfield, London. Their dog won't go down to their lower cellar, no matter how hard they try to coax it. Its hair rises. Further more, it often cries in sympathy when either its master or mistress goes down there.

But the dog might only be sounding a warning bell of things about to happen. Glasses, cups and other breakables simply rise up, leap off the tables and crash onto the floor. In bed at night, Mark and Lisa can hear loud banging coming from the same place – the lower cellar. It's Mark who usually does the investigation. But just before he opens the cellar door, the noise stops. It might have sounded like 100 party-goers whooping it up. But as soon as anybody is about to go in, the noise stops. Just like that.

And it isn't only Lisa and Mark who have problems with ghosts in the pub. Here is what Mark said to me about another ghost:

One day when I had just opened the pub, my chef came to ask me if the elderly lady was going to order some food. I told her (my chef) that there was no one in the pub besides ourselves. But chef said there was. She had just seen an old lady through the glass window in the kitchen door. Chef said: 'She was wearing a blue cloak and her grey hair was tied up in a bun'. She was that precise. We walked into the area together and there was nobody there. I checked the toilets and all over but there was nobody in the pub besides ourselves.

My team also say they have seen a human figure or a light passing through the figure in the lower cellar. Things disappear and turn up in another place. An old employee told me he saw a previous chef outside the kitchen door and he had seen a figure in the garden when there was nobody there either. The pub wasn't even open.

Back In 1977, in Andrew's *Phantom Ladies*, the then licensees, Ray and Sue Williamson, had a similar problem, not only with their dog but their cat as well. Neither would go into the cellar. Their hair would bristle. From time to time, Ray also complained about the ghostly chill down there.

Other spooky problems were a ringing of the 'time' bell – well before 'time' – and the experience by a customer, Brian Bullock, of 'the vague figure of a little old lady passing one of the windows', when in fact the pub was empty. In February 1976, Sue told Andrew that doors continued to bang mysteriously and weird footsteps were heard.

Back in the nineteenth century, there were two murders associated with this pub. The body of John Draper was found at the bottom of a nearby well in 1816. Benjamin Danby, a sailor, was murdered there in 1832. A former landlord, James Tuck, was charged with murder, but the evidence was not strong enough to convict him.

Whatever thing from heaven or from hell has been haunting the Crown and Horseshoes for so long? (Did some one say, 'ask the dog?')

CROWN AND HORSESHOES
HORSESHOE LANE, ENFIELD, LONDON.
TEL: 02083 631371
OPEN TO THE PUBLIC AT THE APPROPRIATE HOURS

NINETEEN

Norfolk

CASTLE RISING

The mad she-wolf of Castle Rising

In the darkest nights, when the wind rages and werewolves roam the earth, those folk who live near Castle Rising in Norfolk may say softly they have heard the maniacal shrieks of the mad Isabella. Or – when she takes animal form – the howling of the she-wolf.

Isabella was not always mad. She arrived in England at the tender age of twelve; she was to be a bride for King Edward II, well known as a bisexual and more interested in the young men of the court than any woman. But somehow Isabella rose above all this, and for many years she played the role of the perfect wife and mother.

But in 1325, driven to desperation as a result of her loss of liberty, her children, and her income, she somehow managed to escape to France. Here she had an adulterous affair with Roger, Lord Mortimer, an exiled English traitor. Together they managed to obtain a sufficient army for the most successful invasion of England since the Norman Conquest. They deposed Isabella's husband, Edward II, and set themselves up as regents for Isabella's eldest son, Edward III.

Alive, Edward II was a constant reminder that in the eyes of many, he was the true King. He was a problem that had to be solved. For the time being, he had been imprisoned in Berkeley Castle where he was tortured, starved, and held in a damp, dark dungeon. Just below this was a row of putrid animal carcases. The stench can only be imagined. But despite being given the worst of treatments – to the chagrin of his wife and her lover – he continued in robust health.

Isabella and Mortimer gave the orders. He was to be murdered, but no mark must be left on the King's body. No sword thrusts, no ropes. The chosen method of death was considered appropriate for a bi-sexual. This vile choice, invented for the murder, has echoed down the centuries for its cruelty and barbarism. A red-hot poker was thrust up the victim's backside. It is said that his screams could be heard for miles around, by frightened peasants who silently crossed themselves and prayed for Edward's soul.

The true King disposed of, Roger and Isabella now enjoyed a brief period of power before her son, Edward III, came of age and took control in 1330. One of the first things he did was to effect the execution of Mortimer for regicide and the imprisonment of his mother in Castle Rising – for the same crime – where she was kept for some twenty-seven years.

Edward III, still a teenager, had word that Mortimer and Isabella were in Nottingham Castle. The young King and his friends burst into the castle to find Mortimer and Isabella in bed together. They were immediately arrested. Mortimer was executed for treason. Isabella, the Queen, was given a much kinder prison.

Isabella was imprisoned in various castles, her favourite being Castle Rising in Norfolk. She was given every comfort, a court of servants, knights, squires and so on and was also allowed to move about the country, staying in other castles with her large retinue. Part of the conditions of her imprisonment were that she should never show her face anywhere. To this end, it is said she had a tunnel dug between Castle Rising and Red Mount chapel where she could take mass – a round trip of some twelve miles.

But Isabella had a bad press, no less now than in the fourteenth century. In Marlowe's highly acclaimed play, *Edward II*, she was described as the She-Wolf of France and one of the most notorious femme fatales in history. In the 1960 novel, *The She-Wolf of France*, the acclaimed French author, Maurice Druon, describes Isabella as having small, sharp, pointed carnivore teeth like those of a she-wolf. In the mid-nineteenth century, Agnes Strickland writes that:

> *Since the days of Elfrida (who is believed to have arranged the murder of her step-son, King Edward the Martyr in 979) no Queen of England has left so dark a stain on the annals of female royalty as has Isabella. She is the only Queen of England to act in open and shameless violation of the duties of her high vocation. No other queen has allied herself with traitors and foreign agitators against her King and husband, staining her name with the combined crimes of treason, adultery, murder and regicide.*

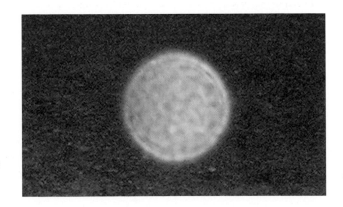

Ghostly orbs – to archaeologist Norman Fahy, who works for the castle, they represent 'the souls of former residents of the castle.

Isabella's shrieks and hysterical cackling emanated from a room in the upper portion of the castle.

And so on and so on. According to popular legend, Isabella's ghost – angry at her critics – can be glimpsed among church ruins, clutching the beating heart of her murdered husband.

Writing in 1973, Andrew gives a brief idea of the location of the castle. The village of Rising once served as a port before Kings Lynn emerged as a rival in the early thirteenth century. The uniquely ornate and spectacular stone Norman keep stands within an oval earthwork which probably dates from Anglo-Saxon times. But it is also an area of known Roman occupation. The earliest stone structure on the site is the Norman church which lies to the north of the castle yard, dating to around 1090, and was built by William D'Albini who was butler to King Henry I.

Lord Howard, owner of Castle Rising, has kindly updated Andrew's work. He writes that Isabella's shrieks and hysterical cackling emanated from a room in the upper portion of the castle. An interesting phenomena is the strange mist coming from the White Room which can form and disappear as quickly as a finger snap, regardless of the temperature or the season. Cooking smells (when nobody is cooking) are also quite common in Castle Rising. The ghost-hunter and barrister, Alan Murdie, has reported to me that in a recent visit to the castle by a young man, there was the distinct sound of children where there were no children.

A new debate has broken out by ghost-hunters everywhere and this is the reports of 'orbs'. Are they supernatural or merely dust particles shown up by the very recent invention of digital cameras? Archaeologist Norman Fahy, of Castle Rising, takes the supernatural line. To him, they represent 'souls of former residents of the castle. He believes in an afterlife and feels privileged to have the faculty to record it.'

Watch these orbs carefully: you might find another manifestation of Isabella the Mad. But which? Perhaps you'll stumble on her as a real live wolf with piercing red eyes and fangs that drip blood. That's Isabella.

CASTLE RISING CASTLE
CASTLE RISING, KING'S LYNN,
NORFOLK, PE31 6AH
TEL: 01553 631330.
OPEN TO THE PUBLIC AT THE APPROPRIATE TIMES,
THROUGHOUT THE YEAR. RING FOR DETAILS.

OLD HALL INN

The resident poltergeist

Back in Andrew's 1980 *Ghosts of Today*, he reported finding 'the sweet, sickly smell of strong tobacco.' Today, Liza Etheridge, the present publican, tells me about the same thing – the sweet, sickly smell of strong tobacco. Liza also tells me of frequent poltergeist activity in the manager's flat above the pub. On numerous occasions, the occupants returned to the flat to find ornaments turned round and their pet teddy bear standing on its head.

Andrew found more. He writes that there is a recorded drop in temperature when the figure of a woman in grey clothing is seen sitting on a window ledge in the television room. At 11 o'clock one morning, the manager's wife saw 'a column of grey smoke move across the dining room towards the kitchen.' This was witnessed on separate occasions, by other people.

Andrew was always very keen on testing the supposed paranormal whenever he could, and he reported it to a team of researchers from the Borderline Science Investigation Group (BSIG) who came to the conclusion that this 400-year-old building was genuinely haunted. The publican knew that already. It was haunted in Andrew's time. It is haunted now. (BSIG is now defunct. Andrew enjoyed being its president.)

THE OLD HALL INN
THE COAST ROAD, SEA PALLING,
NORFOLK NR12 0TZ
TEL: 01692 598323
OPEN AT THE APPROPRIATE HOURS

TWENTY

Northamptonshire

------◆◆◆◆◆------------------◆◆◆◆◆------

THE SAMUEL PEPYS COUNTRY PUB

Poltergeist in the pub

When Andrew was writing about this small country hotel back in the 1970s, the then publican Harry Rogers complained about shuffling footsteps in an empty room above the bar, objects jumping around and a ghost that was terrifying his young son. This ghost was described as 'a little old lady in a blue frock'.

When I contacted the new publican, Fraser Williams, he told me they had experienced similar trouble, but there was also a new ghost. This unnamed spirit appeared in the Back Bar shortly after midnight, dressed in a white night gown and carrying a candle.

THE SAMUEL PEPYS COUNTRY PUB AND DINING
SLIPTON, NORTHAMPTONSHIRE, NN14 3AR,
TEL: 01832 731739
OPEN TO THE PUBLIC AT THE APPROPRIATE TIMES

TALBOT HOTEL

Ghostly meeting with a five-year-old

'It was not a 'real' person; the five-year-old boy confessed to his mum. And his mother later took it up with Bruno Mollier, manager of the Talbot Hotel in Oundle. It was a recent Sunday morning and the young lad had spotted the ghost (for that was what it must have been) from the landing window of one of the bedrooms on the second floor. The apparition was standing on the staircase. The boy called his mother. She came to the window but couldn't see anything. It must have been her son's private phantom.

'So it was my chance,' Bruno told me recently, 'to give her some inkling of the famous ghost of the Talbot Hotel.'

Andrew told that story back in 1977 in his *Phantom Ladies*. He wrote that guests had complained about an inexplicable drop in temperature in a particular bedroom and of being disturbed by a 'peculiar wailing' in the early hours which could not be associated with the central heating or staff working. Other hotel guests had remarked on the sounds of a lady walking along the carpeted corridor late at night. One man was more than a little shocked to hear footsteps walking past him when there was nothing to see.

A few people enquired about the cries of distress that sounded like a woman sobbing which came from the room next to the 'cold area'. The room was always empty on these occasions.

There are not many people who have seen the phantom – the five-year-old being the exception. One witness though saw a woman in the reception area and she was able to describe her: 'she was wearing a fawn coloured skirt with what looked like a white blouse and a cap. But when I enquired as to the name of the guest, I was told the hotel was empty that evening.'

The ghost has occasionally been seen looking down into the yard from a window on the landing. She can now be easily recognised by her small cap and white blouse. It's a pity no one quizzed the small boy as to what his private ghost was wearing.

TALBOT HOTEL
OUNDLE, NORTHAMPTONSHIRE, PE8 4EA.
TEL: 01832 273621
OPEN TO THE PUBLIC AT APPROPRIATE TIMES

TWENTY-ONE

Northern Ireland

ANTRIM CASTLE

An annual haunting

Antrim Castle Gardens are one of only a handful of late seventeenth-century Anglo-Dutch water gardens surviving in the British Isles, and one of only two left in Ireland with their original features and layout. The castle, which was home to the Viscounts Massereene and Ferrard, was gutted by fire in October 1922, and the ruin finally demolished in the 1960s.

*Antrim Castle – put
31 May in your diary now.*

Legend has it that on 31 May each year a large ghostly coach with four fine horses can be seen galloping down from the castle straight into the long pond where the combined apparition sinks out of sight.

This is really an annual renactment of what happened here three centuries ago when a drunken coachman late one night mistook the moonlit waters for the road surface and plunged himself and his passengers into a cold, wet grave. I have been unable to obtain the exact year in the eighteenth century when this unfortunate drowning took place. I see Andrew, writing in 1973, was also unable to give the year. I doubt if anyone does know.

ANTRIM CASTLE
COUNTY ANTRIM, NORTHERN IRELAND
PUBLIC ADMISSION AT THE APPROPRIATE TIMES
TEL: 02894 481338

BALLYGALLY CASTLE HOTEL

A rather solid type of ghost

There is your will-o'-the-wisp type of ghost. Just some kind of amorphous mist or even of a definite shape. If you can get close enough and put your hand out, it will go right through it. Then there is the other kind.

Take this ghost, seen recently in the Ballygally Castle Hotel. Peggy Brown, the housekeeper, was cleaning the floor when, in her own words: 'Someone grabbed me by the shoulders and pushed me right through the room and into the bathroom. I said: "Stop it Mrs Maud", thinking it was my friend. But even if it had been my friend, I would have been amazed at the unexpected force of the blow.'

But it was not Mrs Maud. 'I looked around to see if I would find anybody. I was alone. If it were a ghost, which seemed very likely, it was the most amazing ghost I've every experienced. And I'm no lightweight.'

But there were other ghosts Peggy Brown had known and others' experiences at the hotel too. One girl was offered a tidy sum to stay by herself in the haunted room for the night. She stayed till about 2.30 a.m. Then it got quiet and eerie. The floorboards starting creaking and she left.

Ghostly things continued to happen. Peggy Brown, responsible for cleaning room 44, found one peculiarity. Here it is just as it happened. 'Every time we came to clean this room, we found the water glass upside down over the plughole of the sink, even though we had left it upright on the shelf the day before. If it had broken, it would have ended up another way, so someone must have moved it'.

Ballygally through the arch.

'This happened every night for about six weeks, and then one day we left it in the sink just as it was, upturned. Next morning, it was in the same position. We put it back on the shelf and it never moved again.'

Other things started to happen. In some rooms, lavatories flushed by themselves, bedclothes turned down and turned up without assistance: then a waiter came in early in the morning to hear the piano playing in the lounge. He went to investigate. Who could be playing at this hour of the morning? He was beginning to feel extremely angry. Well, he found the piano playing all right – but nobody was playing it. He began to feel jumpy.

Ghosts at Ballygally have been around for the best part of 400 years. The popular idea is that one of the ghost is that of Lady Isobella Shaw, wife of Lord James Shaw. Lord Shaw wanted a son, and when his wife delivered a girl, he snatched the baby from his wife and locked her in a room at the top of the castle. The story doesn't explain what happened to the unfortunate baby but goes on to say that trying to search for her beloved child, Lady Isobella fell to her death from the tower window. Another story is that she was thrown from the window by the cruel Lord Shaw or one of his henchmen.

Lady Isobella's ghost is thought to be a friendly ghost who walks the corridors of the old castle. Over the years many guests have reported strange experiences and have felt a presence in their rooms. There are endless stories of unexplained noises in the night, and an eerie green mist over the castle. There is even a designated Ghost Room in one of the towers in the oldest part of the castle.

Ballygally landscape.

Reports of a ghost in the old building commenced shortly after the death of a Mrs Nixon, of County Fermanah in the eighteenth century. The owner of Ballygally at that time, Henry Shaw, had married a daughter of a Sir John Hamilton. Two sisters of the new Mrs Shaw, both childless widows, Lady Slane and Mrs Nixon, came to live with them at Ballygally. Because this so enlarged the Shaw family, it became necessary to build additional accommodation for them and their servants. This became the west wing and also known as 'Madam Nixon's Room.'

Much of Mrs Nixon's time was spent in the castle and when she died there her apparition in a silken grey dress was seen walking the passages at night, amusing herself by knocking at the doors of different rooms. Although she is no longer seen in the hotel, numerous guests have heard footsteps walking in the upstairs corridors and must have been puzzled by hearing loud knocks on their bedroom doors – when opened immediately, only an empty passageway was to be seen.

There is one thing to be thankful for. Most of the ghosts here have been gentle and misty. Not at all like the solid brute who shoved Peggy Brown so very hard!

BALLYGALLY CASTLE HOTEL
BALLYGALLY HEAD, CO. ANTRIM,
NORTHERN IRELAND, PT40 2QZ.
TEL: 02828 581066.
OPEN TO THE PUBLIC AT THE APPROPRIATE HOURS.

SPRINGHILL

A pact with the dead

This is the story of a couple who made a pact in life which could only be answered by the ghost of whoever died first. This is one of two strange stories connected with this grand old Irish house, Springhill. I'll begin with the first story, which I think is the more unusual. However, this one left no haunting behind. It is a fantasy, a dream, the essential details written down over a century after the events took place. It is a fascinating ghost story, nonetheless.

A brief word about Springhill itself. This is a seventeenth-century plantation house, now belonging to the National Trust, but formerly the home to ten generations of the Lenox-Conyngham family. It has a walled garden, a fine library, and is widely recognised as having Ireland's best documented ghost.

This first story concerns Sophie Nichola Hamilton, related by marriage to the Lenox-Conynghams, and the youthful Lord Tyrone. As youngsters, they spent much time in each other's company and were under the care of 'persons who educated them in the principles of Deism.' Being so close and deep believers in their faith, they made an extraordinary pact: 'Whoever should die first, he or she would, if possible, appear after death to the other and declare what religion was most approved of by the Supreme Being.'

After Sophie's marriage to Sir Tristram Beresford, and Lord Tyrone's union with a Miss Rickards, 'no change of circumstances or condition diminished their former friendship.' Their families often visited each other, spending upwards of a fortnight together each time.

Then something occurred that would shake the faith of the most earnest ghost-hunter. If you do not find this story credible, then many would ask: what ghost stories are? Like religion, they rely on faith. It was a few months before the birth of Sophie's son. She and her husband, Sir Tristram, were on a visit to Gill Hall, near Dromore in County Down.

Sophie woke one night to find Lord Tyrone sitting by her bedside. She screamed and tried to wake Sir Tristram but he was dead to the world after an evening of too much good wine and brandy. The phantom spoke:

> *Have you forgotten your promise? I died last Tuesday at four o'clock and have been permitted by the Supreme Being to appear to you to assure you that the revealed religion is the only true one by which we can be saved. I am also permitted to inform you that ere long you will have a son, which it is decreed shall marry my daughter. Not long after this child's birth, Sir Tristram will die, and you will marry again to a man whose ill-treatment will render you miserable and you will die in the 47th year of your age.'*

Lady Tristram asked if Lord Tyrone was happy? He answered, 'Had it been otherwise I should not be permitted to appear to you.' Sophie asked if he could give her some proof that this had not all been a dream. The late Lord Tyrone waved his hands and the bed curtains were instantly drawn through a large iron hoop. He also wrote in her pocket-book in his old familiar handwriting. But Sophie persisted. She said she could have performed these actions in her sleep, she wanted ever more proof.

He touched her wrist. His hand was as cold as marble, and in a moment 'the sinews of her wrist shrunk up.' The phantom then gave her a command: 'While you live no mortal eye must behold this wrist.' At this point, Sophie fainted.

The next morning, seeing her husband was already up, she replaced the curtains. She also locked up her pocket book and bound a black ribbon around her charred wrist. On rejoining her husband, Sophie managed to persuade him never to inquire why she wore a black ribbon and also told him that they would soon hear word that Lord Tyrone had died. At that moment, a servant brought a sealed letter, edged in black.

As the years rolled by, every one of the phantom's prophesises came true. After Sir Tristram's death in 1701, Sophie kept to herself, shunning society, always conscious of the unhappy consequences should she marry again. But despite this, she was somehow persuaded to marry a man much younger than herself in 1704. But the phantom's predictions continued to come true, including her new husband's behaviour: he proved to be 'the person destined by fate to be her undoing'.

She took no joy in becoming forty-seven, the predicted year of her death. But, to her relief, the fatal year passed without disaster and she was much cheered. On her next birthday, the clergyman who had baptised her came to her in good spirits. He had been checking the parish records and told her the records were wrong. He congratulated her that she was a year younger than she thought. 'You are but forty-seven today.' Ashen faced, she turned toward the good clergyman and told him: 'you have just signed my death warrant.'

She invited her son and good friends and told them the story of the predictions, and how they had all come true, including the black band around her wrist. She said goodbye to her guests and retired to her bedroom. With her last breath, she rang her bell violently. Those guests that hadn't left the house came to her bedside. The servants were dismissed, and someone removed the black band from her wrist. Underneath, it was as Sophie had described – 'every nerve withered, every sinew shrunk.' She then died as it had been forecast.

The next ghost story concerns Olivia Irvine of Castle Irvine, who lived and died at Springhill. She was married to George Lenox-Conyngham – his second marriage, and from all accounts, not a happy one. Up to that time, around 1816, Springhill had been a family residence for the same family for over 300 years, and had no reason to be considered haunted.

Springhill, scene of some of the most extraordinary ghost stories in Irish history. (courtesy of the National Trust)

In 1816, George Lenox-Conyngham committed suicide following severe depression. He was sixty-three. A contributing factor was that Olivia was somewhat less than a sympathetic and loving wife. For all that, Olivia followed her husband to the grave in 1832. And all ghostly manifestations seem to date from about this time.

The first incident involved the dead George's son-in-law, Andrew Stuart. He had been given the Blue Room, and one night before turning in, he had arranged his clothes tidily on a chair. When he awoke the following morning, he found that his clothes had jumped onto another chair.

The family entertained a great deal and often Springhill would be full of family and friends. In 1888, a Miss Wilson, a close friend of Millie, the elder daughter of the house, was a guest. That night, Millie joined Miss Wilson in her room and the two friends chatted until the early hours when Millie returned to her own room. This was the Cedar Room, halfway up the main staircase. After she had gone, Miss Wilson found that Millie had left her diary behind. Knowing that Millie would need the diary, she hurried up the stairs to the Cedar Room, on to the landing. .

As she did so, she saw in the bright moonlight streaming through the landing window, a tall woman whom she did not recognise, standing on the upper landing. The ghost (for it seems that was what it was) appeared most distressed and hurried across the landing to the door of the Blue Bedroom, whereupon she flung her hands in the air and promptly vanished. Only later was Miss Wilson able to recognise the ghost from a family portrait. She was the dead Olivia Lenox-Conyngham.

Many generations later, it seems that the ghost of Olivia appeared in the same Blue Bedroom, where this time, two small boys were sleeping. They told their nurse that 'a lady stood at the mantelpiece and talked to them.' The boys were not at all frightened by the behaviour of the ghost and this tied in with what was known of the long dead Olivia and her love of children. Single-handedly, in the flesh, she had nursed a family of six through the dreaded smallpox.

A very curious manifestation took place in this room in the last decade of the nineteenth century. A guest by the name of Miss Hamilton came down to breakfast one morning, pale and upset. Her tale, told word for word, in Mina Lenox-Conygham's *An Old Ulster House*, had Miss Hamilton saying:

> *I had gone to bed in the great four-poster and the fire had died down and I had begun to feel drowsy when it suddenly seemed that the room was full of excited people – servants I thought – who were pushing and wrangling in whispers. I felt I had overcome fear, but then I heard a clicking sound behind me, as though a door had been opened and then a light shone at my back, and someone seemed to come through this light and still the commotion, so all fear left me, and after a while I fell asleep…*

Years later, in the 1980s, the Lexon-Conynghams long gone, another child told of a 'grey lady' who touched her arm (a flesh and blood touch?) while she was on the upper landing. One or two of the children of the family also mentioned 'a gentleman in a cloak' in the Blue Room who, it seemed, they did not like one little bit!

There have been all kinds of disturbances at the house in recent times. Commonly mentioned have been the usual footsteps in the attics. An old oak cradle has been known to move, as if by an unseen hand. There is one place in Springhill that is supposed to exude an indefinable sense of dread. This is one of the outside sheds and someone recently confessed that it gave him 'the shivers'. Anywhere in the house and grounds you can, from time to time, feel the 'presence' of Olivia.

The present property manager of Springhill, Patricia Law, has seen Olivia on a number of occasions and is able to give a good description of her. She is a tall, dark-haired woman in a black dress with her black hair tied up in a bun. She is a happy, friendly spirit who seems to love children. But Ms Law is of the opinion that she is also highly strung. There is some speculation as to why Olivia does the haunting and not her husband who was, after all, the one who committed suicide. Or was it suicide? Only the ghosts know for sure.

SPRINGHILL
MONEYMORE, CO. LONDONDERRY.
NORTHERN IRELAND
OPEN TO THE PUBLIC AT THE APPROPRIATE TIMES
TELEPHONE: 02886 748210

TWENTY-TWO

Northumberland

CRASTER TOWER

The great tower mystery (or was it poltergeist?)

I'll have to leave most of this to Andrew. There has been little change in Craster Tower except that there are now three flats there rather than just three rooms in around 36sq. ft. It's still owned by the Craster family and the great puzzle remains. The earliest part of the Tower dates from 1290, but the modern part dates from 1730. It is only about 65ft high.

Now, to the mystery. Sir John Craster (who died in 1976) was coming down for breakfast one autumn morning when the maid asked him to go into the dining room 'before she moves anything.' In his own book, *North Country Squire*, Sir John writes 'of two big and heavy china vases, on each side of the mantelpiece, that on the left as one faced it was broken in half, with the upper part lying horizontally where it had stood and the other half, unbroken in the fender. Behind the fire-screen was an uneven shaped heap of soot.

'The nearest inside window seat was a good five yards distant and there was not a scrap of soot between this and the heap in the fender; and yet on the window seat was the perfect outline of a naked human foot in soot, and just one foot at that.' This was not the only incident in the tower, but was the only one of its type. Other phenomena heard by both Sir John and his wife when in the front library have been 'strange bangings and things coming from the wall dividing the front from the back libraries.' The Crasters point out that the noises are certainly not made by rodents, and having become accustomed to them, the family merely accept them as 'one more unsolved mystery.'

The best-known phantom of the Tower is that of the grey lady who has been witnessed by dozens of people over the years. James Wentworth Day in a *Ghost-Hunter's Game Book* tells of when his young daughter in August 1955 enquired about the woman 'who opened the front door, came upstairs and went into the drawing room.' James himself heard and saw nothing but 'a presence was definitely there.'

Fairly recently, Sir John's sister heard a coach and horses come along the drive and to the front door. It was night but everything was brilliantly lit by the moon

– though nothing was to be seen. After a few minutes, the invisible carriage was heard to move again and drive round to the stables at the back of the house.

The phantom lady is seldom seen, but more often heard, by the sound of her rustling skirts. According to one witness, 'she comes in by the first floor front landing window, moves slowly towards the pele tower and then vanishes.'

Recently, heavy footsteps have been heard coming up the stairs at a time when there was nobody there. (And even this, I am told, may have been when the hostess was rather generous with the wine).

Craster is on a small road running along the edge of the coast and is only two miles from Dunstanburgh Castle, which is open to the public and under the guardianship of English Heritage. Craster Tower is of course entirely private and not open to the public except by writing to the Craster family at the Tower.

CRASTER TOWER
CRASTER, ALNICK, NORTHUMBERLAND, NE66 3SS
OPEN TO THE PUBLIC BY APPOINTMENT ONLY. PLEASE RESPECT

LINDISFARNE PRIORY

Lindisfarne Priory, situated off the Northumberland coast and linked to the mainland by a tidal causeway, is situated on Holy Island, which became a cradle for the nurturing of Christianity in these parts. The site is one of the most important early centres of Christianity in Anglo-Saxon England. It has also been a place of myths and miracles for a thousand years. Chief among those spreading the holy word was St Cuthbert, whose ghost must surely be the most revered in the country. He has often been seen in the Norman priory and by the rocks known as St Cuthbert's Beads. These are actually fossil Crinoid Columnals but legend has it that St Cuthbert made them, sitting on one rock and using another as an anvil.

The sound of hammering heard at night is attributed to the saint working away at making his giant rosary beads. Sir Walter Scott, source of a myriad of quotations, used this myth in his epic poem, *Marmion*, describing how the nuns at Whitby Abbey were intrigued by the story:

> *On a rock by Lindisfarne*
> *St Cuthbert sits and toils to frame*
> *The sea-born beads that bear his name;*
> *Such tales had Whitby's fishers told*

Northumberland

And said they might his shape behold,
And hear his anvil sound;
A deafening clang – a huge dim form
Seen but, and heard, when gathering storm
And nights were closing round.

Lindisfarne became an important centre of learning in Anglo-Saxon Britain. There is some dispute among scholars as to where precisely Christianity first arrived in the country but St Aiden – whom many believe was the first to spread the good word – came to the priory in AD635 and is buried here. But the bishop who came after him, St Cuthbert, is the ghost most frequently seen here and – as I've said – most revered.

Before coming to Holy Island, Cuthbert had joined Melrose Abbey in the Scottish Borders and then established a new abbey at Ripon, in North Yorkshire, preaching to, and in some cases, healing, plague victims. He returned in triumph to Melrose and was named prior. However, he felt drawn to Holy Island, which became his final resting place.

St Cuthbert was once a soldier and his witness to so much blood, death and destruction, led him to being a monk. Before that, he was a shepherd, and it is often said of him that he exchanged his crook for the bishop's mitre.

His must be among the earliest witnessed ghosts, and he is said to have appeared to none other than Alfred the Great – King of England from AD 871 – and foretold his future. Alfred is supposed to have been assured by the same spirit that all would be well, and to have been told (correctly) that he would one day become King of England.

It is claimed that a spectral procession of monks is most often seen by the causeway which links the island to the mainland at low tide. And a monk studiously reading from a parchment has been seen in the ruins. Another ghostly monk stands sentinel by the shore looking out to sea, only to disappear slowly into the sand. It is thought that he is keeping watch in case of attack, as the island suffered relentless raids by the Vikings. The island's isolation had made it a perfect place for a monastery but it also made it vulnerable to attack. In AD 793 legends tell of whirlwinds and dragons appearing in the sky, foretelling the destruction of the early monastery by the Danes. The monks fled, taking the miraculously un-decayed body of St Cuthbert, who had died, AD 687.

They trekked across the north of England in search of a site to found a new community and finally ended their journey at the perfect spot – a rocky outcrop above the River Wear where St Cuthbert was laid to rest and where the monks carried out the foundations of what would later become, under the Normans, one of the most beautiful cathedrals of the world – Durham.

Pat Robinson from Suttons Dwellings, Benwell, said to Andrew in 1967: 'I went to Holy Island for a day last summer and I was having a paddle with the bairn, when I walked past this monk. I even said "Hello" but he didn't answer. He seemed really thoughtful, so I didn't pester him again. I turned around a few moments later to see where he was, and he had just disappeared'.

A string of ghost-monks was witnessed by a number of people walking across the causeway in – 1921, 1933, 1934, 1956, 1981, 1982, 1988 and 1989 (three times). These could be monks on their many pilgrimages; others suggest they are the souls of the monks butchered on the countless Viking raids that plundered Lindisfarne. It may, on the other hand, be nothing other than a lot of tourists with over-active imaginations.

Andrew, writing in 1973, says that the monastery, founded in the seventh century, was destroyed by the Vikings, but the Normans rebuilt it as a priory. Andrew was also intrigued by the 'spine-chilling names' of the Vikings He cited Eric Bloodaxe, Ivor the Boneless and so on. In Andrew's day, Lindisfarne was owned by the Department of the Environment; it is now in the care of English Heritage. He recorded his thoughts when he visited the island in the 1970s. 'Walking across the sands to the ancient rocks on which the impressive castle and priory stand can easily fill one's mind with mental pictures of the terror-stricken monks rushing across the beach with their valuables pursued by the bearded men of the north. Swords flashing, battle axes swinging and the cries of victory as the Norsemen capture a monk or kill a fleeing abbot. Much of the treasure from the priory was, in fact, saved but at the cost of many lives.'

St Cuthbert's ghost has been seen on a number of occasions in the priory. He was spotted by eight choirboys as they were rehearsing. Scared, they all scattered amongst the pews. But according to the islanders, St Cuthbert can be seen at any time when the moon is full, and the tide is about to roll across the causeway. The saint is always somewhere on the island.

LINDISFARNE PRIORY
HOLY ISLAND, BERWICK-UPON-TWEED,
NORTHUMBERLAND, TD15 2RX.
TEL: 01289 389200.
OPEN TO THE PUBLIC AT THE APPROPRIATE TIMES. TELEPHONE FOR DETAILS.

THE LORD CREWE ARMS HOTEL

Ghosts that brought 'a feeling of tranquillity'

Dorothy Forster is the chief resident ghost at the Lord Crewe Arms Hotel in Blanchland and she appeared in 1988, just as new owners were moving in. 'She doesn't like change', the old owner told newcomers Alex Todd and Peter Gingell. 'She will play up until you settle in.' Sure enough, Dorothy played her little tricks. It was harmless but quite enough to annoy. A fire door which cannot be locked, refused to budge. 'You have to be patient with Dorothy,' Alex and Peter were reminded. Within a few minutes the door opened like magic.

'There was another little trick', Alex told me. A member of staff was checking the linen in the restaurant when she was aware of a 'presence' in the room. (Anyone even remotely aware of ghosts will recognise that word). Where once there had been a doorway was now a cupboard. The staff member felt an icy chill as Dorothy swept past her through the cupboard.

A honeymoon couple were staying in the oldest part of the hotel. During the night, they were woken by a cold, grey mist ballooning towards them. They'd heard of the ghosts of the Lord Crewe (Dorothy again?) and felt no fear. They were simply aware of that 'presence' again.

Hotel staff and guests talk. Dorothy will often be 'felt' on the ancient stone staircase leading to the restaurant and other rooms. This frequently gives people a feeling of not being alone, an awareness of some one else being with you and the usual cold draught of air. That's what they say.

Dorothy shows no sign of jealousy. But she is not alone. There's also a red haired, bearded monk dressed in a white habit who shares the limelight. Guests get rather alarmed to wake and see him kneeling beside their bed in prayer. Well, you would get something of a shock, wouldn't you? But somehow not so. For everyone reports a feeling of tranquillity. Nobody has reported fear. And the only guest who has ever asked to change rooms has been a priest! One wonders if it was because of Dorothy or his fellow-in-faith, the bearded monk.

Dorothy plays her little tricks anywhere.

A view of the hotel and of the entrance to the crypt bar.

But here's a trick right up Dorothy's street (that's if she had one). A chambermaid was cleaning one of the haunted rooms but couldn't keep the plug in the socket on the wall. Seconds after it was plugged in, hey presto! It would jump out again. Thinking it must be the socket, she had it checked. It was found to be in perfect condition. And it just happened to be Halloween.

In 1992 a television crew and six of the country's top psychic investigators set up their equipment in the hotel to see what they could detect. Strangely perhaps, the monk was more evident than Dorothy Forster. The programme was broadcast a few weeks later which delighted all the Lord Crewe staff.

Over the years, the hotel has had many requests from groups and individuals to spend the night at the hotel – particularly at Halloween. They're all here to get a look at Dorothy or perhaps the monk in his smart white robe. And they're not always disappointed.

Andrew, writing in his 1977 *Phantom Ladies*, also knew Dorothy Forster. Not only that; he also writes of the unseen but 'felt' phantom, believed to be the sister of Thomas Forster, in the flesh, one of the plotters of the 1715 rebellion. Thomas was imprisoned but thanks to Dorothy, he escaped and was hidden in a secret room before being smuggled to Europe.

Andrew writes that another ghost is that of Dorothy Forster's aunt but why either should continue to frequent a particular bedroom and other areas is anyone's guess. She was seen in the village square by a vicar and, according to a previous manager of the hotel, 'a large number of other people.' The hotel building is very old. In 1165 it was a monastery, as was most of this small picturesque village. Part of this religious community, founded by White Canons, was sold during the Dissolution. The guest house and kitchen became a manor house and eventually the Lord Crewe Arms Hotel.

THE LORD CREWE ARMS HOTEL
BLANCHLAND, NEAR CONSETT, NORTHUMBERLAND,
TEL: 01434 675251
OPEN AT THE APPROPRIATE HOURS

The ghosts bring a feeling of tranquillity.

TWENTY-THREE

Nottinghamshire

NEWSTEAD ABBEY

Lord Byron and his ghosts

Lord Byron – sometime owner of Newstead Abbey in Nottinghamshire – woke to the sensation of something climbing onto his bed. Something. He felt a light pressure. It took a minute or two to wake up, to focus. The pressure continued. Then, on sitting up, he began to see what it was. The victim of this supernatural creature said later he never missed a heartbeat. But whatever the spectre was, it was getting closer. He was confronted by a shapeless black mass, featureless apart from two red, glowing eyes.

Apparently, the apparition then rolled over and onto the floor and disappeared. It is believed that this 'meeting', (and other confrontations), meant nothing to Lord Byron. But not everyone had his nerve. Byron believed in ghosts and was unaffected by their presence. This ghost story may have been one of many such 'meetings'.

Ghost-Hunter Alan Murdie made a thorough search for the source of this confrontation but could find nothing except a brief reference in a Byron biography that Byron may have seen the Black Friar. Alan also points out that Byron had a sense of humour and this sighting might have been just poetic whimsy.

Newstead Abbey can boast a number of ghosts. Among the best known is the Black Friar, above, who haunts the house as a curse on those who, years ago, made use of property stolen from the church (he has a point). Newstead was of course a monastic establishment before the Reformation, and the abbey church still stands beside the mansion, forming a very beautiful ruin. The Black Friar was thought to be the harbinger of evil to the lords of Newstead. Lord Byron said he saw the apparition just before his marriage to Miss Milbanke, which he always declared was the most unlucky event in his life. He has described the Friar and his curse in these famous lines:

> *… a monk arrayed*
> *In cowl and beads, and dusky garb, appeared*
> *Now in the moonlight, and now lapsed in shade*
> *With steps that trod as heavy, yet unheard…*

Nottinghamshire

...By the marriage bed of their lords, 'tis said
He flits on the bridal eve:
And 'tis held as faith, to their bed of death
He comes – but not to grieve.

When an heir is born, he is heard to mourn
And when aught is to befall
That ancient line, in the pale moonshine,
He walks from hall to hall.
His form you may trace, but not his face,
'Tis shadowed by his cowl:
But his eyes may be seen from the folds between
And they seem of a parted soul.

Byron made a gesture of defiance to the ghost by mounting the skull of a dead monk in silver, then using it as a drinking cup. A writer in 1851 says the cup was first used by Lord Byron at a dinner party. When it had been filled with wine, a headless monk appeared. The ladies screamed, and fainted, but Byron boldly faced the spectre, and challenged it to state its errand. The ghost solemnly warned him to make his peace with God, as he would die young – a prediction that did in fact come true. A visitor to the house, Miss Kitty Parkins, is believed to have seen the Friar, and afterwards made a sketch of it.

It is said that during the Dissolution of the Monasteries, one of the Augustinian Canons (who wore a black habit) would not leave the abbey and Henry VIII's commissioner, Dr London, ordered his execution. It is thought that this is the ghost that has been seen by many people, staff and visitors alike, both in the house and wandering in the grounds.

The Augustinian priory at Newstead was founded in the early 1160s but it wasn't until the Dissolution of the Monasteries in the 1540s that the destruction of the priory church itself took place. Most of the monastic quarters were left standing, including the great hall, the refectory, and the cloisters themselves.

Sir John Byron converted the claustral buildings into his family seat in 1540, but his more famous descendent, Lord Byron, didn't take over Newstead Abbey until 1808 and sold the place to pay off his debts in 1818. The man who bought Newstead was Thomas Wildman, also an ex-Harrovian like Byron, and extremely rich. He lavished money on the estate as if there was no tomorrow. But the improvements outside and in were done with an intelligent flair. And this is broadly what you see today. The abbey house is situated at the centre of over thirty acres of formal gardens and water features.

Another Newstead ghost is 'Sir John the Little with the Great Beard.' That is Sir John Byron, of Colwick, to whom the abbey was granted in the sixteenth century. There was formerly a portrait of him on the wall, and the figure was said to descend from its frame at midnight. One visitor said she saw him in daylight, when reading a book by the fire. Andrew described him as the 'only genuine phantom which is known to exist here.'

A third ghost is one of several White Ladies. She is supposed to be a sister of Lord Byron's immediate predecessor in the estate. This is the infamous 'Devil Byron,' who was put on trial in 1765 for killing a Mr Chayworth in a quarrel, which he said was a duel. He was a wild and unstable character, and did his utmost to destroy his heritage, so that the estate should have little value to his successor.

He had a violent quarrel with his sister and refused to speak to her for some years before her death. He paid no attention to her pathetic appeals. 'Speak to me my lord, do speak to me.'

Washington Irving tells a story of a young lady, sleeping in the abbey, who saw the White Lady come out of the wall on one side of the room and go into the wall on the other side. It's the sort of thing ghosts do very well.

There is another rather sad White Lady who was deaf and unable to speak. She was the granddaughter of the Honourable William Byron, but a daughter of whom? Here was the rub. Her mother had committed the very worst crime for a near Honourable. She had married beneath her – to one of the estate's dog-keepers, strictly against her father's wishes. Sophia, who became the White Lady, was the product of that liaison.

Sofia felt drawn to Newstead Abbey and she was taken in by one of the adjacent farms. She spent her time writing poetry about Lord Byron and wandering the abbey grounds, always dressed in white with a veil covering her face. (Thus, the White Lady).

She comes into the picture at the time when Lord Byron had sold the estate to his very rich old school friend, Thomas Wildman. Sophia Hyatt was a devoted fan of the poet and his work but her disability had left her shy and withdrawn. She avoided contact with strangers and would go so far as to dive into a nearby bush when she saw anybody approaching. If contact was unavoidable, she would always carry a slate on which to write.

When the Wildmans, the new owners of Newstead Abbey, learned of her fondness for Byron's work, they gave orders that she be allowed to wander the grounds of the abbey when ever she chose. She used to take the abbey dog – a descendant of Byron's Boatswain – on walkies.

Throughout her life, she had been given money to live on by a relative, and in 1825, the relative died and the money dried up. Sophie had another relation in America and she was determined to ask them for help. She set off for Nottingham aiming to take the stagecoach to London.

She left a letter with the Wildmans telling them of her plans. Mrs Wildman read the note and showed it to her husband. They immediately dispatched a rider to overtake Sophia, offering her free accommodation in the grounds of Newstead for the rest of her life. The rider set off in hot pursuit and on reaching the market square, saw a large crowd gathered around a horse and cart outside the Black Boy pub. The rider dismounted and pushed through the people to find Sophia lying on the ground – dead. She had been run over by a cart, not hearing the drayman's warning. She was buried in Hucknall, not far from Lord Byron's grave.

The grand façade of the old abbey. (courtesy of the Nottingham Museums, Galleries and Heritage)

Today, she can be seen wandering around her favourite gardens at Newstead. She particularly favours one path which has been named after her – the White Lady. She is remembered again in the abbey restaurant – also called the White Lady. Susan Patching, one of the senior guides in Newstead Abbey today, says she has often been told of sightings of Sophia, often by the waterfall. A visitor once showed her a photograph of the waterfall, with an outline of a white shape in the waterfall itself – and it certainly looked like a lady. A white lady.

Staff at Newstead like to put on a ghosts' show, dressing up to play the part. On one particular night, one of the ghosts put up an even better show. As the visitors were passing the bottom of the staircase, a strong smell of roses and lavender invaded their senses. The Rose Lady (I've lost count of the number of ghosts we're up to) had won the day. As ghosts always seem to, don't you think?

NEWSTEAD ABBEY
NEWSTEAD ABBEY PARK, RAVENSHEAD,
NOTTINGHAMSHIRE NG15 8NA.
TEL: 01623 455900.
OPEN TO THE PUBLIC AT THE APPROPRIATE HOURS.

TWENTY-FOUR

Oxfordshire

THE GEORGE HOTEL

A good hard thump in the back (just when you're settling down to sleep)

She didn't scream, she just cried. Louise Collis and her husband had recently gone to the George Hotel in Dorchester-on-Thames, on the spur of the moment – for a change of scene. Well, Mrs Collis got rather more than she had bargained for. They were not even allocated a known haunted room (for the hotel is famous for its ghosts).

Mrs Collis tells the story in her own words:

We retired to bed around midnight and quickly fell asleep. My husband snores and on occasions keeps me awake. I was asleep when I was woken by three loud bangs on the wall – not sure which wall. As I woke up, I heard my husband snoring loudly, so thought the bangs must come from disgruntled visitors in the next room. Worried about this, I lay in bed nudging my husband every time he started snoring. This went on for a while until I eventually closed my eyes to rest.

I was in this twilight state not really asleep and not really awake when I felt a sort of lump appear in the mattress underneath me. I was thinking: 'what is that?' when all of a sudden I felt a hefty blow to the centre of my back where the lump was. This was quickly followed by a tingling sensation over the whole of my body. I couldn't breath or move. I tried to call out to my husband but just had a gurgling sound in my throat.

It sounds really bizarre but I felt like someone/something was inside my body. After only what seemed like a few seconds, I managed to move my leg and actually kicked my husband. He in turn pushed me and whoever/whatever was in me left through the front of my body and I heard it go through the door – at least the door rattled as if someone had banged against it. I sat up and turned on the light. I was totally breathless and very scared. I was crying and had the feeling that I had to leave the room immediately. I asked my husband to check the time – it was 3.30 a.m. In spite of my fears we did not leave, although I did not sleep for the rest of the night and we left at 8.00 a.m. When we left we found that there was no room next to ours.

Other hotel guests have written in to the George with their stories. This one is from Brendan Kennedy who has a request for the hotel.

A lot of holding people down in their beds. And still they come… guests as well as ghosties.

I stayed at the George Hotel in Dorchester this weekend and I think I have been lucky enough to experience some paranormal activity… which may be confirmed by the fact that I have videoed about ten orbs in my bedroom and I didn't even realize until I played the video back last night for the first time. Therefore, would love to go back to the George if you will be arranging a special weekend there.

Author's note. Orbs – round bubbles of light or dust particles – are viewed by different people with dissimilar views. Some believe that they are precursors to the appearance of people-ghosts, others that they are evidence of an after-life – a kind of ghost. And others still believe they only started to be noticed after the invention of the digital camera.

Another guest, Adi Howson, is also interested in orbs.

I stayed (in the hotel) last Friday night (30 June), room eight, where my wife-to-be and I took some photos of the room. We have one photo with three clear orbs showing, possibly more, as I haven't studied it closely yet. It was also very hot in the room – a fact the maid made a point of telling us – which is strange as the room doesn't get direct sunlight.

The final report comes from Mike and Michelle Menhennett, appointed new managers at the end of 2006.

My family and I moved into the George Hotel on 4 December 2006. We stayed in room eleven, one of the outside rooms on the balcony. It was the first night of our stay in this room. I woke up at about 4 a.m. as I could see the clock-radio. I was unable to move any part of my body apart from my eyes and I could see a circle of what looked like smoke in front of the door; it did not make me feel really scared until I tried to move to wake up my husband, but then I went back to sleep.

Two weeks ago in room three, my sister and her husband, who had not been told about my experience, ran into the same problem, of being held down on the bed at different times of the night, once with the lights on. The other interesting thing is they had the bedroom windows open all night and did not even once hear the abbey clock bells which are unmissable and ring at every quarter of the hour.

The George Hotel, built in 1495, is a delightful, old, half-timbered coaching inn with oak beams and inglenook fireplaces throughout. Set in the heart of Oxfordshire, it provides seventeen en-suite bedrooms, some haunted.

Andrew, in *Phantom Ladies*, notes that the George stands on the site of an inn which was probably the ale house for the monks of the nearby abbey. He also makes three ghostly references: one is to a 'miserable young woman'; the second was seen in 1971 in what was the 'Vicar's Room'; The third was a white-gowned phantom who 'stands at the foot of the bed contemplating the occupant/occupants.' Andrew speculates that the ghost looks with such sadness towards the bed before she turns and vanishes, the probable cause was that a loved one had died under tragic circumstances in the bed that existed there at the time. Andrew always was a romantic.

THE GEORGE HOTEL
HIGH STREET, DORCHESTER-ON-THAMES,
OXFORDSHIRE OX10 7HH
TEL: 01865 340404.
OPEN TO GUESTS AT THE APPROPRIATE HOURS

KENTON THEATRE

An adopted fifty-year-old ghost

The principal ghost in Henley's Kenton Theatre, (built 1805), was hanged half a century earlier, in 1752, and there is no knowledge that she haunted anywhere else first. Mary Blandy faced the final penalty for poisoning her father. From all accounts, she was a good looking girl and came from a different class of woman than those usually sentenced to face 'the drop'. She was middle class and well educated for the time. Her father, Francis, was a prosperous lawyer and the town clerk of Henley-on-Thames. Mary's is an interesting story and worth a few lines here. I should also add that the haunting of the Kenton Theatre was made a close study by the Ghost Club Society in 2004 and I'll give their main findings later in this entry.

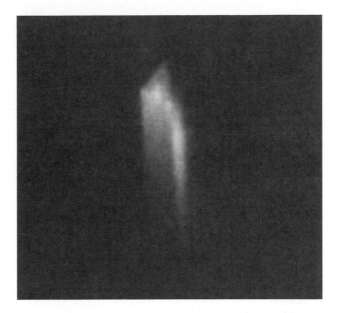

Supposed ghost of Mary Blandy. Photograph taken in total darkness. (courtesy of Trevor Kenward)

Mary Blandy's family lived a comfortable life but the event that precipitated the road to the gallows was a newspaper advertisement put in by her father, Francis. It offered a £10,000 dowry for his daughter's hand in marriage, an enormous sum in the middle of the eigthteenth century. All suitors were rejected except one, the Honourable Captain William Henry Cranstoun, son of a Scottish nobleman. He was therefore acceptable by birth, but after he had been living in the Blandy household for over a year, the real Cranstoun began to be revealed. Francis, but not his daughter, seems to have seen the young man for what he was. To cap everything else, it was discovered that he already had a wife in Scotland.

Realising that her father had cottoned on to him, Cranstoun persuaded Mary to administer what he described to be a 'love philtre' to her father. This, he assured her, would change Francis' hostile attitude towards him. Mary was completely fooled by this nonsense and didn't realize that the so-called love potion she dished out to her father was really arsenic. What she doesn't seem to have realised either was that her boyfriend (they weren't married yet) would do anything to get his grubby fingers on her £10,000 dowry. Ironically, her father's estate came to little more than £4,000 but, under the laws of the time – had she married her so-called boyfriend, the £4,000 would nevertheless automatically pass to him.

Over the weeks, Mary – blissfully unaware of what she was doing – cheerfully mixed in the arsenic with her father's tea and gruel. Even watching him slowly getting sicker and sicker, she didn't suspect anything. The servants, eating a much smaller quantity of the poison left on the food, were only mildly affected. Even this didn't raise Mary's suspicions.

When her father was obviously nearing death, Mary called in a physician who advised her that she would be held responsible for her father's death from arsenic poisoning. Desperate to save her skin, she burned Cranstoun's love letters and also attempted to burn the poison.

Susan Gunnel, the housemaid, had the presence of mind to rescue some of the unburned powder from the fireplace and had it analysed. The chemist advised her that the powder was in fact arsenic, a slow killer. But either Mary wasn't told or simply didn't register. To the very end, she didn't connect the 'sprinkle' put on her father's food and his severe illness. Even when her father was on his deathbed, Mary still hadn't realised that she was, in fact, his murderer.

The wheels of the law grind exceeding slow and it was some time before she was arrested. As soon as Cranstoun got wind of this, he abandoned her, and Mary was left to face trial and execution by herself. On the day of execution, her last request – 'for the sake of decency gentlemen, don't hang me high' – was allowed (otherwise, it was thought, the young men at the hanging – and there was a large crowd – could have looked up her skirts).

It is interesting to note that the ghostly disturbances at the Kenton Theatre appear to have been sparked off by the restless ghost of Mary Blandy. She gained notoriety as a ghost in 1969 when Joan Morgan's play, *The Hanging Wood*, was being staged at the theatre. The play covered the life and death of Mary.

Inexplicable bangs and lights switched on and off were amongst the phenomena experienced. The spirit of a young woman made an appearance (was it Mary?) but perhaps the climax was the levitation of a tea cup which rose by itself then crashed on to the floor.

The Kenton Theatre is ranked as the fourth oldest working theatre in the country and has a rich and varied past. Aside from its function as a theatre, the Kenton Theatre has been a congregational church, a school, a wash house for beer barrels and a warehouse for storing scenery. It has been reopened twice, once in 1926 – and then closed in 1963 (for failing fire regulations) – only to open again in 1967 thanks to a group of volunteers. Since this time – and according to the ghost report mentioned earlier – the theatre has proceeded to quietly prosper as a centre for amateur dramatics.

The theatre has been visited previously by members of the Ghost Club Society and has a reputation for being haunted. Some of the spooky events which happened here are listed below.

A director and three actresses were rehearsing on stage when a female apparition appeared at the back of the hall and walked across the back of the stands, then through the opposite far back wall. A workman, sawing on the stage area one evening, halted his work and noticed that the sound of the sawing continued – echoed by a phantom carpenter perhaps? An apparition of a woman walked down the dressing room stairs and then simply vanished. We have already listed this one – lights have gone on and off, unaided.

An interesting side note to the story is that for a period of a few months before the death of Mr Francis Blandy, the house had been plagued with unexpected phenomena. There had been unexplained music in the parlour room, and bangs, raps, rustling noises, and footfalls. Cranstoun himself claimed that at one point he had been visited by the doppelganger of Mr Blandy himself.

Andrew, writing in 1980, says that the ghost [he doesn't say which one] was seen once or twice in 1969 by members of the cast during rehearsals, seen again at the back of the stalls, and over a mirror in a dressing room. He adds that things were 'mysteriously moved.' The more imaginative believe Mary is responsible.

So Mary has the last line after all.

KENTON THEATRE
NEW STREET, HENLEY-ON-THAMES,
OXFORDSHIRE, RG9 2BP,
TEL: 01491 575698
OPEN TO THE PUBLIC AT THE APPROPRIATE TIMES

TWENTY-FIVE

Scotland

CRATHES CASTLE

Phew! What a smelly ghost!

It's mainly the stench of tobacco that has been detected all over Crathes Castle. But there have also been other smells such as egg, lamp oil and soot. Nobody – either visitors or staff – has been able to provide any explanation. Other ghosts have been seen rather than smelt. Most often seen is that of a young woman, sometimes carrying a baby or small child in her arms.

The origins of the Crathes' ghosts are told by Andrew in *Our Haunted Kingdom* and the story is a very familiar one. Some time in the seventeenth or early eighteenth centuries, a laird's ward disgraced the family name by becoming pregnant by a local ghille. We know the servant was immediately dismissed but the fate of the young woman is only guessed at. Then, 150 years on, during modernization, the pitiful skeletons of a baby and its mother were discovered – the child under the hearthstone of the fireplace.

One of the finest examples of a Jacobean castle in Scotland. Pity about the hanky-panky.

For many years the Green Lady's Room has had a reputation of being haunted by the spectre of a young woman who made her first appearance to the 4th baronet in the early eighteenth century. Whether it was on account of seeing this spectre or for other reasons, the baronet developed an obsessive fear of ghosts. Today's visitors to the castle often claim to have seen the spectre of a young woman.

Crathes Castle is thought to be one of the finest examples of a Jacobean castle in Scotland. It dates from 1553 and was given into the safekeeping of the National Trust for Scotland in 1951. Built in typical baronial style, it has a magnificent Great Hall with a carved granite fireplace, views over the spectacular gardens, and some rather weird painted ceilings with a mixture of grotesque faces, strange designs, and appropriate advice such as 'File sone all naughtie companie' and 'From fools no friendship crave'. But catch that ghost and you'll reach for your handkerchief. The staff can only say sorry.

CRATHES CASTLE
NEAR BANCHORY, KINCARDINSHIRE, SCOTLAND
TEL: 01330 844525
PROPERTY OPEN ALL YEAR ROUND
18 MILES WEST OF ABERDEEN AND
NORTH-WEST OF STONEHAVEN

CULZEAN CASTLE

A feeling of uneasiness and dread

A group of ghost-hunters recently reported back on their experiences in Culzean Castle in Scotland. The headline illustrates their fears. They approached the 1777 castle in pitch darkness, 'jumpy' right from the start. Margo, author of the report, tells us it is a place populated by spirits (she says she actually sees them lined up in expectation of her visit) and is a place to test your metal. In four closely typed pages, she recounts her group's exploration of the castle. Right from the start, she feels that her group are about to experience 'a very eventful evening'.

They explore the balcony, where Margo has to overcome her dry-mouth-fear of heights. She suddenly feels she is too close to the edge. Then life turns into a movie. A thriller. She can see – though no-one else in the group can – two spirits fighting. One is bigger, stronger than the other and the stronger pushes his fellow-spirit off the edge. To his death. That was how it seemed to the Margo – but can a spirit actually die?

Inside the castle, she feels 'extremely uneasy and nauseous.' She is 'light headed' with a 'heaviness on my back and shoulders'. Another member of her group feels 'dizzy and unwell', Margo senses 'a lost spirit wandering around, going around in circles, confused and exhausted'. She somehow sees herself in that spirit.

In another part of the castle, Margo hears a baby cry. She asks one of the group, Frances, if she had heard it. Nobody else had at that moment. The group also visited the Ailsa suite, a room Margo had disliked on a previous visit. Here she senses – almost sees – a spirit standing next to the bed.

They hold a séance in the dining room. Margo's group prays, lights candles, hears tapping, smells gas [there were no gas connections in the building] then rotten fish. But after a while, Margo stops the séance abruptly. Why? She gives an explanation: she was 'nauseous, weepy, felt the temperature plummet, she was shivering'. That explanation will have to do for the moment.

In Andrew's idea of life and death, there were no séances, no spirits. He believed in no after-life, no heaven, no hell. However, like an old trooper ghost-hunter, he would have liked to hear what Margo and her group had experienced.

Andrew described Culzean castle in *Ghosts of Today*. He tells of its dramatic position overlooking the Firth of Clyde. He also reports that back in 1976, two of the many visitors to the castle saw a 'peculiar misty shape' travelling up the stairway – something that has been seen on a number of occasions since.

CULZEAN CASTLE
MAYBOLE, STRATHCLYDE ,
SOUTH AYRSHIRE, SCOTLAND,.
TEL: 08701 181945
OPEN TO THE PUBLIC AT APPROPRIATE HOURS

DUNTRUNE CASTLE

The ghost with no fingers

He didn't start with no fingers. The piper who was to become a ghost was born with the full set like you and me. But the fingers that played the pipes so beautifully, were to be sacrificed for the lives of his fellow men at arms. It was clan against clan; this time the Campbells were the enemy. No Campbell or his property was secure from these raiders.

According to Andrew, the story really begins in the seventeenth century with Ulster Macdonnel Coll Ciotach, 'The Left-Handed One.' His forces – our piper amongst them – landed in Kintyre, a southern peninsula of Argyllshire, and marched north, ravaging people and, ransacking property as they went. They also had a ship close at hand, on the loch and both forces would soon come to within striking distance of the Campbell's great castle, Duntrune, facing Loch Crinan.

Wanting to establish the strength of the castle's defences, the Left-Handed-One sent our piper as a spy to find out how easy it would be to attack Duntrune Castle by land and by sea.

The spy managed to get easy access to the castle but was almost immediately suspected of being up to no good. Suspicions, however, couldn't have been very high for our piper was confined, not in a dark, damp dungeon, but in one of the turrets where he had panoramic views over the loch.

From this vantage point, he spotted one of his own ships clearly heading towards Duntrune Castle. The piper had had enough time to realise the strength of the heavily defended castle and knew that somehow he must warn his fellow men-at-arms that it was almost impregnable.

The Campbells were spoiling for a fight – a fight he knew they would probably win. But how could he escape and give warning? Then he hit on a plan, a simple and effective way to win the day. Choosing a spot in the turret where the sound of his pipes could most easily be heard, he played the pibroch – the piper's warning to his master.

Today, the family 'pleasantly share the castle' with their ghost.

But as he saw clearly that his plan had worked, he also realised that he had just signed his own death warrant. Seeing that his ship now headed away from Duntroon, back to the Emerald Isle, he braced himself for the torture that would most surely be his punishment. Now he would experience the dungeon and the torture chamber. Cutting off his fingers – with which he played so beautifully – must have been merely a preliminary for what he was now about to face. Perhaps he realised it then – that soon he would be a ghost.

For many years the sound of his pipes have haunted the castle. In the 1880s, an important discovery was made. It happened purely by accident: when some building work was being carried out, a skeleton was discovered whose fingers had been hacked off. He had been entombed in the old walls.

The occupier at the time, an Episcopal clergyman, was asked to give the remains a Christian burial to 'lay the spirit'. This rite was carried out and the ghost, who had been regularly appearing in the castle, was thought to have now been exorcised. But in 1972, the then owner, Colonel G.I. Malcolm of Poltalloch, told Andrew that certain evidences of the spirit could still be seen and heard. 'Strange knockings on doors when nobody was without, pictures falling for no reason', and, on one occasion, 'several heavy pewter objects thrown to the floor by unseen hands.' They were the hands of a poltergeist.

Today, the castle is still standing, defiantly looking out over the loch and the land, and occupied by Robert Neill Malcolm, chief of the Malcolm/McCallum clan. Colonel Malcolm has his own ideas as to why the piper continues to haunt the castle. Could it be, he thinks, that the piper was a Macdonell or a Macdonald and therefore more than likely to be a member of the Catholic faith? If this was the case, being buried in the wrong churchyard may have disturbed the piper's spirit and his peace of mind.

He thinks the piper was a MacDonald [though perhaps he might have been a hired musician and thus belonging to another family, possibly Macintyre.] These things, in those days, might have given the Campbells an additional reason [as if they needed one] to execute him.

Mr Malcolm told me that nowadays they pleasantly share the castle with the piper and welcome his benign presence. In a personal view he says the piper's activities were triggered 'by a dislike of my step-mother who would never spend a night alone here – something that has never worried anyone else in the family.'

Duntrune is a magnificent example of a twelfth-century Scottish baronial castle, situated close to the end of the Crinan Canal and slightly north of the lighthouse. Built on a solid granite foundation it faces over the waters of Loch Crinan and beyond to the Sound of Jura on the west coast of Scotland.

Andrew writes that the castle is set in the glorious landscape of Argyllshire, the fortress standing proudly and even loftily on a small peak in its own estate. Originally it was a lonely fortress guarding the rich mainland from marauders, but in the sixteenth century a dwelling house was constructed using the original keep, with another floor added, incorporated into its massive stone walls.

Up to 1797, Duntrune was the seat of the Campbells [now Inverary] but their neighbour, Malcolm of Poltalloch, bought it when the trustees of the last owner offered it on the market. For such an ancient structure it is unusual that there is so little recorded history. No one has any knowledge of who built it or exactly when it was built. One of the few details that are known is linked with the no-fingered, friendly ghost that continues to haunt this ancient fort and share the space with its amused (and equally friendly) inhabitants.

DUNTRUNE CASTLE
LOCHGILPHEAD, ARGYLLSHIRE,
SCOTLAND, PA31 8QQ (OFF THE B2085)
OPEN TO THE PUBLIC BY APPOINTMENT ONLY

INVERAWE HOUSE

The roof came off and the ghosts came out

That was more or less how Mrs Campbell-Preston, of Inverawe House, described her haunting to me. The centuries-old manor house was getting a new roof over the kitchen and as soon as the old one was off, certain 'things' started to crawl out. A student, Linette, staying at that time in the kitchen wing, was on her way to the loo in the middle of the night when she was startled to see an apparition. It was a maid or housekeeper with long fair hair and a full old-fashioned dress. Linette saw it disappear through a wall before she realised it was a phantom. She was then so frightened she swore she'd never go into the loo again (a vow I imagine she didn't keep for very long!). Then, when a new roof was put on, there were (almost) no more ghosts. Mrs Campbell-Preston still senses an invisible presence from time to time. Or is it the wind, she ponders? In her view, maybe a lot of paranormal activity could be explained away, but not all. 'I can't believe that everything seen by rational, intelligent people can be made up.'

She cites a happening which was experienced long ago by her bridge partner in India. As children, they naturally looked for other children to play with. Then one day new children did appear on the scene and they were invited over. But as those children approached, they simply faded away.

Andrew wrote quite a lot about Inverawe House in *Our Haunted Kingdom*, after he had interviewed the present owner's father. The manor house is situated amongst the magnificent scenery of the Pass of Brander in the rugged solitude of Argyllshire, and overlooked only by the 3,700 ft high Ben Cruachan.

The Campbells have been associated with Inverawe House for some 400 years and in a 1951 privately published history of the family, the author writes: 'On the assumption that the first Inverawe was a son of Sir Neil of Lochow who died before 1316 and had married the sister of King Robert Bruce… this family would be the oldest branch of Argyll still to hold the name of Campbell.'

The previous Mrs Campbell-Preston told Andrew that although neither she nor her-son-in-law had seen or heard any ghostly manifestations, her ten-year-old grandson 'senses' things in this house.

While I was researching for this entry, a helpful librarian in the area sent me a copy of a ghost story connected with Duncan Campbell of Inverawe. 'It is interesting', the story goes, 'because the characters, places, and events are real and authenticated'. Despite the comment, the story does not have the ring of truth. It is probably fictional, but I'm including it because it's a good, interesting yarn.

The ancient castle of Inverawe stands in the midst of the wild and picturesque scenery of the Western Highlands. The time was before the middle of the nineteenth century. Late one evening, the laird, Duncan Campbell, sat alone in the hall of his castle. There was a loud knocking at the gate. Opening it, he saw a stranger with torn clothing, and kilt besmeared with blood. In a breathless voice, the stranger begged for asylum.

He went on to say that he had killed a man in an affray and that his pursuers were at his heels. Campbell promised to shelter him. 'Swear on your dirk!' the stranger said, and Campbell swore. He then led the stranger to a secret recess in the depths of the castle. Scarcely was the stranger hidden when there was again a loud knocking at the gate and two armed men appeared. 'Your cousin Donald has been murdered and we are looking for the murderer!' Campbell being true to his oath professed to have no knowledge of the fugitive, and the men went on their way.

Then the laird, greatly agitated, lay down to rest in a large, dark room where at length he fell asleep. Waking suddenly, in bewilderment and terror, he saw the ghost of the murdered Donald standing by his bedside and heard a hollow voice pronounce the words, 'Inverawe! Inverawe! Blood has been shed. Shield not the murderer.'

In the morning, Campbell went to the hiding place of the guilty man and told him that he could harbour him no longer. 'You have sworn on your dirk', the stranger replied and the laird of Inverawe, greatly perplexed and troubled, made a compromise between conflicting duties. He promised not to betray his guest, but led him out of the castle to the neighbouring mountain (Ben Cruachan) and hid him in a cave.

The next night, as Campbell lay tossing in feverish slumbers, the same stern voice awoke him. The ghost of his cousin, Donald, stood again at his bedside – and again Campbell heard the same appalling words, 'Inverawe! Inverawe! Blood has been shed. Shield not the murderer!'

At break of day Campbell hastened to the cave but it was empty: the stranger had gone. That night, as he strove in vain to sleep, the vision appeared once more, ghastly pale, but less stern in aspect than before. 'Farewell, till we meet at TICONDEROGA!'

This strange name dwelt in Campbell's memory. He had joined the Black Watch, or 42nd Regiment, then employed in keeping order in the turbulent Highlands. In time, he became its major and — a year or two after the American war broke out — he went with the regiment to America. Here, to his horror, he learned that his regiment was ordered to the attack of Ticonderoga. Campbell's story of the ghost of Donald was well known among his fellow officers. They pondered long and hard as to how to bring relief to their troubled fellow officer. How could they disarm his fears? When they reached the fatal spot they told him on the eve of the battle, 'This is not Ticonderoga. We are not there yet, this is Fort George.' But in the morning, he came to them with haggard looks.

'I have seen him! You have deceived me! He came to my tent last night. This is Ticonderoga! I shall die today!' His prediction was fulfilled.

INVERAWE HOUSE
INVERAWE, TAYNUILT, ARGYLLSHIRE, SCOTLAND
PRIVATE PROPERTY. PLEASE RESPECT

STIRLING CASTLE

Footsteps in the dark

It scared the living daylights out of Gary D'Arcy, a senior steward at Stirling Castle. You'd think he would have been used to the castle ghosts: they do have a good number. He goes to investigate a blackout in the Ephinstone Tower. The lights go out once and he resets them. The tower lights then go out again. Was it a practical joke? He braces himself to hear the mocking laughter. But all he hears in the total blackness and absolute silence is the sound of footsteps.

He counts them 1...2...3..., he waits: then, he keeps counting, they are getting closer. Nearer ...11...12... the footsteps continue. Then they stop right in front of him. But he sees nothing. Hears nothing. Gary doesn't wait for more. In his own words, he said 'I don't skip, I don't walk. I don't jump, I run. I run like hell just to get out of there.' He feels the sweat on his forehead dribbling down his face, his heart trying to beat out of his chest — and he keeps running. Gary has never been so close to a ghost before. He never wants to be again.

That all happened to Gary in 2005. There are other ghosts in Stirling Castle, several, but not all, seen within the last twenty-five years. The Green Lady, perhaps the Castle's most famous ghost, was last seen back in 1996. She has walked the passages for centuries but her appearances have had dreadful significance. She is perhaps an early warning system of approaching fire.

One night, when Mary, Queen of Scots and her entourage were staying at Stirling Castle, her personal attendant had a premonition that the Queen was in danger. She rose from her bed and raced towards the royal apartments where she found the Queen surrounded by a ring of fire – a candle had caught the draperies around the four-poster and everything was alight. The attendant, who was about to reach the spirit world, was of course the Green Lady. But if the attendant suffered death, the Queen was rescued. Mary later recalled that there had been a prophecy that the Queen's life would be in danger from fire while staying at Stirling Castle. It really was a bit late!

Another sighting, undated, occurred in one of the kitchens. The cook was busy preparing the evening meal when he became aware that he was being watched. On turning round he was startled to see a misty green figure watching his every move. Dinner was late that evening as the cook took such fright that he fainted, knocking over a pan and causing a small fire. Was it the Green Lady heralding another fire?

The next sighting was in 1996 when a contractor was replacing some cobbles in the top square of the castle. Keen to finish the job that day, he continued working until after dark with the help of a small floodlight. He was suddenly aware of some one close by. Assuming it was one of the security staff, he started to chat. Not getting any response, he turned the spotlight upwards. What he saw would have frightened the bravest of individuals: it was a dim green, hooded figure but where there should have been a face, there was blackness. The man ran in terror to the nearest security guard, blubbering with fright. Not ever wanting to go there again – in darkness or in light – he beseeched the guard to retrieve his tools. Well, there was no fire that time.

Next in our gallery of ghosts is the Pink Lady. She is known to walk between the castle and the church of the Holy Rood. She was the daughter of the Castle Governor, betrothed to an officer stationed in the castle. When her fiancé was accidentally killed by her father, she threw herself from the battlements onto the rocks below as she was unable to face the world without her lover.

In another story concerning the Pink Lady, she is the wife of a soldier. When he is killed during a castle siege, she dies of a broken heart. As a phantom, she roams the ground between the castle and the graves. According to legend, she is forever searching for her lost lover.

There are several stories concerning the King's Own Buildings, commonly known as the Governor's Block. In 1946, a new officer was billeted in a room at the top of the building. He complained of frequent use of the outside spiral staircase leading to the room above. He was told that there was no outside staircase nor any room above his. The same complaint was lodged by a major in 1956. This man had seen action all over the world and was not one to be alarmed easily. Nevertheless, he chose to be billeted with his men rather than have to stay in that room another night.

In the regimental history, a curious incident is recorded that may be connected with the heavy footsteps. In the 1820s, there was a 'sentry beat' along the battlements that existed at that time above the Governor's Block. One night a sentry who was taking over guard duty from a previous guardsman found him dead at his post, slouched on the ground, mouth open, with the look of abject terror on his face. There is no explanation, no medical record, just a note of several subsequent 'disciplinary cases' before sentry duty above the Governor's Block was discontinued.

The Regimental Ghost of Stirling Castle. Taken by an experienced but unknown photographer, the image of the ghost in highland dress was a surprise to everyone when the film was published. (courtesy of the Museum of the Argyle and Sutherland Highlanders)

There have been other reports of mystery footsteps. Early morning cleaners reported hearing footsteps running along a corridor from one end of the building to the other – but this did not add up as the longest corridor only ran half the length of the building. It was later discovered that at one time there had been a corridor running the full length of the building.

We now come to the Ephinstone Tower, reputedly the most evil and haunted place in Stirling Castle. This is thought to have been the torture chamber from where, some say, the screams of the tormented could be heard all over the castle. There is an odd story that James V kept Siamese twins here, locked up 'as an oracle.' After the first twin died, the surviving one had to live with his brother's rotting corpse until his own death ten months later. One night a security guard was on patrol here and on this particular night, he also brought his dog along. Nothing could persuade the dog to enter. The poor animal waited outside, his hair standing up on end. A psychic recently visited the Elphinstone Tower but she too would not enter. She became ashen-faced and said she felt an evil presence. There was no joy and happiness here, she said.

This last tale about the tower involved a visit from two boys and their father. He told the boys, aged around five, to stay in the widest part of the tower, or alternately, squeeze themselves against the wall to let others pass. Later, seeing them following his advice so precisely, he asked what they were doing. 'Just what you asked us to do Dad. Letting somebody go by. But nobody had passed him. The father asked the boys what the person looked like. They described a man in funny 'old fashioned clothes'. The father quizzed the boys further and it emerged that the man could have been wearing a ruff round his neck. With a little more questioning, the father was sure it was a ghost – but an Elizabethan one.

During the summer months the castle plays host to many different acts, put on in what they called the Palace. One performance in particular, a one-man-act, was staged a few years ago and attracted good audiences – possibly because of its ghostly content. After one showing, a woman in the audience asked who the supporting actor was. This was a one-man show, she was told. But she was convinced there was a second actor standing behind the 'solo-performer'.

The woman left but she returned a few minutes later; she led the actor to the next room, to a portrait on the wall. 'That's him,' she said. 'That's the man who was behind you during your performance.' The portrait was of James V but – very unusually – with no hat. 'What's the King like,' he asked. 'Thinning on top', she answered. After considerable research, the actor later verified that everything she had said about James V was correct. The ghost must have been none other than the King himself – James V.

The ghost of a woman has been seen in the Palace by two different people in the same place. A female security guard was inspecting the ladies' loo when she was startled to see – reflected in the mirror – a woman standing behind her. But when she turned around in a panic, there was no one there.

There were two sightings of the next ghost, seen way back in the 1930s and this ghost wears a kilt. Some pictures were taken by an architectural photographer. He arrived at the castle just after dawn, planning to photograph the castle site with no people to get in the way. He took a number of shots, packed up and left, sending the film away to be processed. When the prints arrived, he was annoyed to find someone else in the shot, a man in a kilt – a ghost in a kilt.

An article appeared in a local paper and in response to this the photographer received a number of letters. One read as follows:

> I was very interested to read the article about what must be a ghost. There is a ghost of a kilted figure that haunts Stirling Castle and I have seen it myself while I was doing my recruit training in the winter of 1952.
>
> The figure you show is going up into the top square to the Chapel Royal. On the morning I saw it, I was entering the square from the opposite direction through the archway from the Douglas Gardens. It passed along the wall of the Kings Old Buildings and disappeared in an angle created by a tower housing the Regimental Sergeant Major's office in those days. There is no doorway here.
>
> The soldier next to me in the ranks on that cold winter's morning was a complete stranger, but he had also been observing this strange apparition. When it disappeared we both turned to each other and exclaimed: 'Where did it go?'

There were other goings on in the Great Hall during its restoration in 1999. Workman complained of 'something' trying to get past them on the spiral staircase. A couple of them had even been pushed!

Back in 1980, Andrew seems to have been short of space in his *Ghosts of Today*. He does refer briefly to the Pink Lady but otherwise talks about the dramatic location of Stirling Castle. 'Standing on a sheer two-hundred-and-fifty-feet crag of solid basalt overlooking the Forth Valley.' The castle was built and added to at various times, mostly in the sixteenth and eighteen centuries. Other things of interest are the crowning of Mary Queen of Scots in the Chapel Royal in the castle.

Stirling Castle is reputedly Britain's most haunted castle. Well, you certainly get a lot for your money, even if the ghosts don't appear at your bidding.

STIRLING CASTLE
CASTLE WYND, CASTLE WYND. STIRLING,
SCOTLAND, FK8 1FJ.
TEL: 01786 450000
OPEN TO THE PUBLIC AT APPROPRIATE TIMES

TWENTY-SIX

Shropshire

❧━━━━━━━━━━━━━━━━━━━━━━━━━❧

FEATHERS HOTEL

The pretty girl in a micro-skirt and a see-through blouse

It's an old, old story but well worth repeating. During the summer of 1974, Mr Ainsley, a commercial traveller, had an appointment at the seventeenth-century Feathers Hotel in Ludlow – but he was unfamiliar with the town. As a result, he was a few minutes late in arriving and irritated with the parking problems. However, after touring round a couple of times he was very lucky to find a parking place right opposite the entrance of the hotel.

He pulled up, grabbed his briefcase and was already halfway across the pavement when he remembered he had forgotten some important papers. He turned to retrieve

Sorry, the girl-ghost doesn't come with the hotel. We can, however, promise you a lot of haunting.

them from his car when he saw the figure of an attractive young girl, aged about sixteen, with a daring mini-skirt and a blouse that left little to the imagination. Stopped in his tracks, Mr Ainsley was agog. He then saw this young dream of a girl walk straight through his car, glide onto the pavement and vanish from his life forever.

Hardly able to believe what he had seen and bursting to tell someone the story, Mr Ainsley rushed into the Feather's bar and collapsed onto a chair next to the counter. Before he had could spill out his story, the barman greeted him with a smile. 'Good afternoon sir,' he said. 'I know exactly what you've seen – a young girl showing more than she should gliding through your car. Here's a brandy. It's on the house.'

Mr Ainsley discussed the incident but there was little more he could find out at that time. The girl had been seen several times, always at the same place, usually about midday, and wearing the same clothing.

Andrew acknowledges his source. It was a Birmingham researcher, Colin Smith, who was able to discover who the girl was – an extraordinary example of a 'ghost of the living' (as Andrew always said, a ghost does not have to be dead). The girl, now in her fifties, would, when young and living in the area, walk through the Bull Ring, at least once a week, to visit her aunt, a Mrs Hughes, who lived near the Feathers. Mrs Hughes and the then teenager were very close. When Mrs Hughes died suddenly, Carole moved from the district to live in Birmingham.

Apart from the hauntings of Carole, there have been a number of other ghostly incidents in the Feathers. These include the ghost of an unknown lady in room 211 with a preference for men – men were the target for most of her hauntings.

In another incident, a couple were in bed when in the middle of the night, the girl woke to find a ghost pulling her hair so hard she was dragged out of bed. Her partner was more fortunate. An unseen hand gently stroked his face. But the torments had not yet ended for the girl. She was too frightened to return to her bed till after day-break, only to find that her nightdress was soaked in water – though the bed and surrounding areas were completely dry.

Perhaps before you tempt the ghosts in the haunted bedrooms, you could not do better than to enquire about the Feather Hotel's Haunted Breaks. These are the result of a life-long interest in the occult by the hotel's founder and the aim is to bring together like-minded people to discuss, experience, and experiment. To help you, there is always an expert team including a psychic and a technician along with professional equipment. You'll also be invited to become involved in group vigils and séances. The evening starts at seven with a fine three-course dinner and ends at 2.30 a.m. after a full English breakfast. Tempted?

FEATHERS HOTEL
BULL RING, LUDLOW, SHROPSHIRE, SY8 1AA.
TEL: 01564 875261.
OPEN TO THE PUBLIC AT APPROPRIATE TIMES

TWENTY-SEVEN

Staffordshire

GLADSTONE POTTERY MUSEUM

The very idea of ghosts is ridiculous

This was the firmly held belief of one of the Gladstone Pottery Museum's staff. The man, whom we shall call John, was quoted in Andrew's popular 1980's *Ghosts of Today*. 'Ghosts don't exist,' John claimed. We've all met people like him. Maybe it's your viewpoint. But the interesting thing about this man was what happened to him after one occurrence.

This is his story. One evening about a quarter to six, John was checking the museum to make sure no visitors had been locked in. He noticed an old man near one of the benches. 'He was grey-haired with side whiskers and wearing a short brown coat like a smock. And as solid as you or me.'

John said. 'I called out to him, pointing out that we were closed. At this, he simply faded away. I found it hard to believe what I had seen.' John checked with other members of staff and found that some had also seen similar phantoms. John was forced to believe what he had seen with his own eyes. It's an interesting case and by no means an isolated one.

All these years later, I checked with the present custodians to see if anyone had seen or heard any more ghostly manifestations. They wrote back to say that ghost-hunting was still a popular sport among staff. In 2006 somebody reported seeing a woman in Victorian dress – she really stood out from the crowd. The museum pointed out to me that they had no logical explanation for her. Again, she was solid, not wispy and ghost-like.

Anything else to back up our belief that the museum is a ghostly hot spot? Well, staff reported pieces of equipment 'moving of their own accord.' Others have 'felt' people standing behind them. Their operations officer is often in the building alone at night and he has heard footsteps coming up the staircase – yet there was nobody else in the museum.

But there are plenty more people out there who do not believe. I suppose that's most of us – until we personally encounter a ghost. Then?

GLADSTONE POTTERY MUSEUM
UTTOXETER ROAD, LONGTON,
STOKE-ON-TRENT, ST3 1PQ.
TEL: 01782 237777.
OPEN TO THE PUBLIC AT APPROPRIATE HOURS.

TWENTY-EIGHT

Surrey

———◆◆◆———————————————◆◆◆———

BROOKLANDS MUSEUM

Dicing with death

From 1906, when the speed limit was an amazing 20 mph, to the end of the Second World War, Brooklands was the exciting home of car and aircraft design. Based at Weybridge, it was the world's first racing and testing circuit. But high speeds inevitably carried a high risk to man and machine and many of these brave drivers now appear at Brooklands as spectres.

One of the most frightening incidents was reported many years ago, but the story is still remembered today. It concerns the twelve-year-old son of a local family, who swore it was true. The lad had recoiled in horror at the figure of an airman staggering around with 'his head hanging off'. The lad was so severely shocked that (according to Andrew) he had to be given medical treatment.

Also seen is the ghost of Captain Troop who went 'over the top of the banking,' racing a Peugeot. But according to local talk, 'it could just as easily have been the ghost of Parry Thomas, who died while attempting a land speed record at Pendine Sands on 1 March 1927.' He lived on the circuit and is buried in Byfleet churchyard.

Another recent ghost was seen by a boy visiting the Brooklands museum with his grandfather, and might have been that of the motorcycle racer, Arthur Moorhouse. And if you take a short walk along the Members Banking to a spot under the Members Bridge, you'll be standing where Brookland's most famous ghost lost his life. Percy Lambert was attempting what was to be his final world record on Halloween 1913. He had promised his fiancé that this was to be his last race when, ironically, he crashed and died.

The first aircraft, built by S.V. Roe, landed on the finishing straight in 1908, and Brooklands developed the land to become a large aircraft manufacturing site. Aircraft such as the Vickers, Wellington and the Hawker Hurricane were built in their thousands during the Second World War and then later came the Vickers Viscount, VC10, Concorde and BAC 1 11, to mention but a few.

Today, ghosts are still seen at Brooklands. After a period of quiet, when the famous racetrack was overgrown and semi-derelict, Brooklands is once again active but in a very different way compared to the past. The popular museum displays a wide range of Brooklands-related motoring and aviation exhibits.

In the winter, ghost-hunting evenings are organised and staff at the museum claim it is Surrey's most haunted venue.

BROOKLANDS MUSEUM
BROOKLANDS ROAD, WEYBRIDGE,
SURREY, KT13 0QN.
TEL: 01932 857381, EXTENSION 246.
OPEN TO THE PUBLIC AT THE APPROPRIATE HOURS

The magnificent men in their plodding machines. (courtesy of Brooklands Museum)

TWENTY-NINE

Tyne & Wear

WASHINGTON OLD HALL

The witch and the chimney sweep

W ashington Old Hall, in Washington Village, Tyne and Wear, is the ancestral home of George Washington, and has a great many American connections. It also has a number of ghosts associated with the house. One is the spectre of a little girl with red hair, seen on the upper landing. She is described as 'a cheeky little thing, quite noisy and likes to jump down the stairs making a noise.'

Washington's local paper, the *Sunderland Echo*, for 30 June 2005, gives the stories of two more ghosts. One story is of a nineteenth-century chimney sweep's boy, who inhabits the nearby pub, the Cross Keys; the other is a so called witch, whom, we are told, appears in the sky over Washington – with or without broomstick!

Washington Old Hall. (courtesy of the National Trust)

The *Echo*'s storyteller styles himself ghost-hunter and the following is a shortened account of these two ghost stories. The first ghost takes us back to the middle of the nineteenth century and the world of the chimney sweeps and the little boys they employed to clean the parts their brush couldn't reach. We are in the Cross Keys, Washington's local, where the ghost-hunter tells the story.

The ghost of the chimney sweep's boy is called Christopher Drummond. He doesn't do anything to frighten you, ghost-hunter says. The ghost of the boy appears in the pub, 'just standing at the bar all quiet like.' For a moment he's there, black with coal dust. Then he vanishes. Ghost-hunter says, 'he can give you a real shock if he takes you by surprise, especially if you've had a few pints.'

The kitchen at Washington Old Hall. (courtesy of the National Trust)

We now turn the clock back to the middle of the nineteenth century to explore what turned Christopher into a ghost. The chimney at Washington Old Hall needed sweeping. It doesn't look much different to any other chimney – simple compared with the complex nature of chimneys in some older houses. But all in all, this was a tough and unhealthy job, with the boy the most affected.

First the chimneysweep pushes his brush up the chimney, not very different from the modern chimney sweep (except of course everything is now electric). A lot of soot comes down but there was still caked on crust that had to be cleaned by hand. Young Christopher was called, and up he went, armed with a brush and metal scraper. The chimney was still warm from a recent fire.

It was the one thing everybody in the business dreaded most. Suddenly, Christopher called down, near panic in his childish trill: 'I'm stuck!'

It was also fatal. This is how ghost-hunter describes it. 'It took a lot of time and effort to get Christopher Drummond free. And when they did get him down, he was at death's door. So they brought him down to the Cross Keys pub, thinking that fresh air and a nip of brandy might sort him out. They laid him out round the back, but it did him no good and the poor lad died.'

But young Christopher did not die in vain. The newspapers took up the story and it got national attention. Giving in to public pressure, the government passed an Act of Parliament that banned children from working as chimney sweeps. Actually there were a series of Acts from 1840 to 1875, the last being a total ban.

Ghost-hunter was about to leave the Cross Keys when a young woman came bustling up. 'You're after ghosts, then?' she asked. Ghost-hunter confirmed that he was. 'Well then, come here.' The young woman stepped outside the pub door and pointed to the war memorial a short distance away. 'That's where they killed the old witch way back. People reckon you see her late at night, flying above us. Are you interested? You should be. Look up… in the sky.' Perhaps not surprisingly, there was nothing there.

A couple of days later, ghost-hunter called in to Sunderland Library to find out if there had been a witch executed at Washington. He guessed there would have been and that it should have taken place in the seventeenth century – and so it was.

In 1676, a strange murrain killed all the cattle in Washington village. What this strange livestock disease might have been is unclear, but it was very deadly. Living on the outskirts of the village at the time was a bad-tempered old widow named Jane Atkinson. She did not get on well with her neighbours and had often threatened them with unspecified disasters after an argument.

The villagers took it into their heads that the old woman was a witch and that she had been responsible for the disease. They took her to the village pond, on the green where the war memorial now stands, and bound her hand and foot. According to the superstitions of the time, the devil would save his own. If they threw her into the pond, the devil would make her float if she were a witch, but let her sink if she was a good Christian. To avoid killing an innocent suspect, it was usual to tie a rope to the accused's waist so she could be hauled up if she sank.

Tied and bound, Jane Atkinson was tossed into the pond. She sank. The vicar ordered that she be brought back up and she was, but as the poor woman lay gasping on the grass, the villagers argued that it had not been a fair trial. There had not been time for the Devil to do his work. Jane Atkinson was thrown back. She sank again and the villagers were so convinced of her guilt that they gave the Devil plenty of time.

By the time the vicar had persuaded them to haul her up, Jane Atkinson was dead. Even so, she was pronounced guilty by the villagers.

So, supposedly, there was truth in the story about the witch done to death in Washington. And it seems some people claimed to have seen the witch in spectral form, as alleged. Wait long enough into the night, they say, and you will see the witch flying through the night sky silhouetted against the moon. It's a lovely picture, if only it were true.

The above outlines the stories we know about haunted Washington Old Hall. However, there have been two recent paranormal investigations, the first by Most Haunted in 2004 and Haunted North East in 2006. These investigations have resulted in the following disclosures. So far, we have only the headings but sadly, not the full stories.

A man and woman in the bedroom who are never there at the same time. because they don't get on.
A woodcutter on the stairs.
An elderly woman in a rocking chair..
Extreme changes in temperature.
Motion sensors being set off when they hadn't been switched on.
One of those working in Washington Old Hall felt tugging at her belt, and was shaken by the experience.

Andrew, writing in 1973, gives some links between Washington Old Hall and the United States. In Buckinghamshire, for example, he says there is the Mayflower Barn, said to be built from the timbers of the pilgrim's ship. Northamptonshire has the Sulgrave Manor, where a branch of the Washington family lived from 1538 to the seventeenth century, and it was in Nottinghamshire, in a place called Scrooby, where lived one of the Pilgrim Fathers who discussed and planned the famous voyage. Even earlier, another branch of the Washingtons lived here in Washington Old Hall. The Hall became the property of the National Trust in 1956.

WASHINGTON OLD HALL
THE AVENUE, WASHINGTON VILLAGE. DISTRICT 4,
TYNE & WEAR, N38 7LE.
TEL: 01914 166879
OPEN APRIL TO OCTOBER, SUNDAYS TO WEDNESDAYS, 11 A.M. TO 4.30 P.M.

THIRTY

Warwickshire

BROWNSOVER HALL HOTEL

The bottled ghost who changed houses (a most un-ghostly thing to do)

This is the story of a very unusual ghost. He has the odd but descriptive name of One Handed Boughton. More than 200 years before the Brownsover Hall Hotel was built, One Handed Boughton lived in Lawton Hall, a mansion that was later replaced by the building that is now the hotel. Alive, he was a head of a long established local family, but flamboyant, wild and uncontrollable.

His exploits – alive and then as a ghost – were the talk of the town. He would roar about the neighbourhood, terrorising maidservants, chasing nubile local girls and carousing wildly. But here's the interesting bit: most ghosts haunt the premises they inhabited when alive. As a ghost, One Handed Boughton haunted both grand houses, the old and – and many years later – the new, moving from one to the other.

His disability – being one-handed – didn't seem to worry him and it was believed he either lost his hand in an accident or as a punishment for breaking the law. He was summoned for illegally expanding the borders of his land – and may have suffered the barbaric severing of one hand as a punishment.

Sometimes known as the Bottled Ghost, (you'll see why later) his origins are obscure. Some believe that he lived during Elizabethan times, a popular period for the beginnings of many legends: others believe it might have been much earlier. As a ghost, he refused to be confined to Lawford Hall but wandered far afield. For all the world a dashing squire, clad in a red velvet coat, his appearance heralded by shouting and the crack of a whip. He careered through local villages, in a tumbledown coach, leaping gates (a ghost can), driving like the wind, terrifying all who were abroad at the time.

A young man named Aaron Essex encountered One Handed Boughton on a cold September evening in 1710. Essex was walking along the road from Little Lawford to Newbold when he heard the crack of a whip and turning round, saw a carriage and six horses being driven towards him. In the dim light, he couldn't identify the driver but as it reached him, the apparition vanished. For the rest of his life Essex remained adamant that he had seen One Handed Boughton.

This magnificent Grade II Gothic mansion hotel stands mysteriously alone, steeped in its own mysteries.

Early in the eighteenth century, Lawford Hall came into the ownership of Sir Edward Boughton, who had succeeded to the title in 1722. Under Sir Edward, life became more gracious and more sociable. But the activities of the ghost, One Handed Boughton, still continued in and out of his old home, Lawford Hall, and this caused Sir Edward considerable embarrassment. Guests invited to sup with the Baronet hurriedly excused themselves and left the dining table; those invited to remain overnight departed in haste without a backward glance as soon as daylight dawned. Sir Edward's attempts at hospitality were constantly defeated by One Handed Boughton.

By 1752, Sir Edward decided it was time to confront his ghostly ancestor. The situation had become intolerable. He arranged for a group of local clergymen, led by Parson Hall of Harborough Magna, to assist in an exorcism. It was decided to make preparations in the ghost's old bedchamber, the heart of the spectral activities. As they entered the room a violent wind, apparently from nowhere, snuffed out eleven of the twelve exorcism candles. With his colleagues cowering in terror, Parson Hall kept his candle alight long enough 'to conjure the ghost into a green glass phial' which he sealed with a stopper. The phial was then thrown into the murky depths of a clay pit. There is no explanation as to how this capture was accomplished nor whether it would work.

By way of a digression, in 1771 Dowager Lady Boughton's daughter met a Captain John Donellan, fell in love, and a year later, in 1772, they eloped. The family eventually forgave them and they moved back home to Lawford Hall. Lady Boughton's son was a sickly young man who had to take special medicine. He detested the new member of the household, Captain Donellan. One night, after his mother had given him his medicine, he felt worse. The next day he died. A post mortem was held and it was discovered he had been poisoned. To cover his tracks, it was suspected that Captain Donnelan had washed out the medicine bottle to conceal the evidence. Without much ado, the captain was charged with murder and executed in Warwick on 2 April 1781. That's how they did things in those days.

Now, back to our main story of One Handed Boughton. After his exorcism and bottling, the ghost should have stayed in his bottle, but there were still ghostly sightings. Staff reported seeing One Handed Boughton as a dark figure on the stairs at night and servants refused ever to enter the bedchamber. At first, the family tried to keep his bedchamber just as he left it but its evil, oppressive atmosphere terrified all who tried to sleep there. And other manic forces were at work.

At home, in Lawford Hall, One Handed Boughton behaved like a spoilt child. Chairs were overturned, tables moved, things hurled all over the place. He also displayed an action we have observed in other ghosts: his heavy footsteps pounded back and forth. As a result, staff and guests refused to stay and neighbours dreaded going out at night.

In 1790, plans were made to raze the 'accursed' Lawford Hall to the ground – though in practical terms, there was nothing structurally wrong. The family decided to put a stop to all ghostly activities. Ghosts don't change their address, they reasoned – so we'll be rid of One Handed Boughton for good. The hauntings were well known locally and the workmen engaged in the demolition had to be paid extra money to work on the dread site.

True to their plans, a spanking new mansion was built not far from the old site, near Rugby, and called Brownsover Hall. This, essentially, is the exterior which guests of Brownsover Hall Hotel see today. It was designed and built by Sir George Gilbert Scott in a mock Gothic-style with intricate blue brick patterns. The widow of Captain Donnellan married again and the family became the Boughton-Leighs of Brownsover Hall.

One Handed Boughton's ghost seemed to have been finally laid to rest. But early in the nineteenth century, a mysterious bottle was found during drainage work on a pond near the site of the demolished hall.

Legends can be like dreams, with all sorts of twists and turns, sometimes defying logic, at other times ignoring time and dates. It is not unknown to have two or three versions of the same ghost story and there are many different tales about One Handed Boughton. According to Andrew's version, writing in 1980, a fisherman found the bottled ghost in the 1880s. It next appeared in a cupboard in 1964, when Brownsover Hall was used as the head office of the Diesel Engine Division of the English Electric Group of companies. When they left the hall, the bottle was taken by Mrs Boughton-Leigh, a survivor of the original family, who had lived at Lawford Hall.

In 1939, Sir Frank White, father of the modern jet engine, set up a research establishment in the hall with the surviving family occupying part of the mansion. The introduction of modern science had little effect on the old walls. The newcomers, scientists and other workers, all from far afield, knew nothing of the ghostly history of the place. Their whole lives had been spared the antics of One Handed Boughton, yet they now reported many strange happenings, eerie feelings, and the sounds of things going bump in the night.

During the Second World War, like many large houses, Brownsover Hall was requisitioned by the services for valuable research work, although the Boughton-Leigh family remained in a separate part of the mansion. But the haunting continued.

Night watchmen, patrolling the premises after dark, were startled by the sounds of overturning chairs and footsteps emanating from the haunted room, a room they knew to be empty and securely locked. They reported someone or something unseen 'brushing past them' along passages. Pet animals would bristle and refuse to move. A night cleaner swore that he heard talking and groaning from the tower which formed an integral part of the house.

Mr Nairn, a night watchman at the hall, refused to accept that the house was haunted, attributing the noises to the scrabbling of jackdaws in the chimney. His wife, on the other hand, was convinced that the ghost was real. Confirming Mrs Nairn's beliefs is the statement of another night watchman, Mr Dunkley. He had been sitting in the hall one night when he suddenly heard hoofbeats and the sound of wheels on the drive. On opening the front door to see who or what was calling, his dog, Judy, who had accompanied him, snarled, bristled, and fled. The drive was empty.

After the war, the servicemen left the mansion and the Boughton-Leigh family decided to leave too. They sold the big house, initially to become the headquarters and administrative centre of the English Electric Co. – to which I have already referred. Later the mansion became the Brownsover Hall Hotel, which itself has had more than one owner.

But what to do with the bottle containing the spirit of one handed Boughton? The Boughton-Leigh family decided to do away with their ancestor forever.

The bottle was handed over to their agent, who had it buried, deep into concrete, in a secret place which has never been revealed.

But it seems that after all, one handed Boughton has had the last laugh, surviving all attempts to bottle him. Now, half a century on, the Brownsover Hotel is still plagued with ghostly footsteps and groans in the night. Villagers still speak in awe of the coach and six phantom horses racing through the night. I was told that visitors and staff at the Brownsover Hall Hotel fully accept the ghostly happenings as 'one of those things.'

BROWNSOVER HALL HOTEL
BROWNSOVER, NEAR RUGBY, WARWICKSHIRE, CV21 1HU.
TEL: 08706 096104
OPEN TO HOTEL GUESTS AT APPROPRIATE TIMES.

ETTINGTON PARK HOTEL

The most haunted hotel in Britain?

'The Most Haunted Hotel in Britain': that's the headline that stares up at you from various sources, and was first so named by the Automobile Association. From what I've learned of the building, I reckon that it's more than in the running. From the outside, as you approach, you see a brooding neo-Gothic mansion that simply has to be spooked. It was the perfect setting for Robert Wise's classic 1963 horror movie, *The Haunting*, and the ancestral home of the Shirley family for over a thousand years.

Michael Kenny, the former night manager of the hotel, has made it his personal business to investigate and record the various ghosties, who, not surprisingly, appeared to him in the dead of night. A lot of these occurred in the library and I will let Michael tell you in his own words:

I was tidying up in the library when an old book caught my attention. It was a book about the Shirleys and I sat down and started to read. It was about 4 a.m. I had barely started to read when suddenly, I felt someone come from behind me slide their arms over my shoulders and across my chest in what I would describe as a playful and endearing manner.

Initially I was startled and sat bolt upright in my armchair, half expecting a member of staff standing behind me. Almost immediately, however, I totally relaxed again as a warm sensation flooded over and engulfed me. I put my hands up in an automatic reaction to grab the arms folded across my chest.

As I did so, I could feel the hands of a person being slowly withdrawn from across my chest. I could feel the soft, distinctive hands of a lady sliding through mine. The whole experience was a very pleasant one indeed.

So you don't believe in ghosts? Spend a night in this hotel and 'something' will change your mind.

Michael then related the ghostly behaviour of a book from the library. As he was sitting there – it was the middle of the night as usual – a book jumped out of its shelf to crash open on to the floor. It happened several times, and it always was the same book, Sir Walter Scott's *St Ronan's Well*, which always fell open on the same page, carrying a verse by Wordsworth:

> *A merry place, 'tis said in days of yore*
> *But something ails it now – the place is cursed.*

It all gets curiouser and curiouser. Michael goes on to describe his experience with Mary. We do not know a lot about her except that she was a servant girl who died after a fall following an argument she had with a squire. (As these things go with servant girls and squires, you could read a lot into that!) Michael remembered:

The places Mary seemed to like best were the area between the main hotel entrance and the library, and the doorway to the grand Oak Room Restaurant. The hotel dogs, Digby and Molly, would always alert anyone to Mary's presence. They slept under the main stairway. When Mary was present, they would growl, suddenly jump up, and become very agitated. Molly would always rush to a certain spot and stand transfixed, staring intently into the same corner but I could not see or detect any presence. However, I would have to shake Molly to take her out of her trance-like state. The dogs would always settle down again to sleep.

My only altercation with Mary (always assuming it was Mary) happened when I went to close the door to the Oak Room Restaurant. As I pulled the door to close it, it was violently pulled back from me by someone on the other side. I made several attempts to close it but the force pulling from behind was greater than I could manage. Exasperated, I said 'have it your way' and walked away leaving the spot. When I passed the area about twenty minutes later, the door was closed.

But Michael had many more experiences to investigate. He tells the remarkable tale of the moving candle. It was Christmas with sparkling decorations everywhere. Michael was working in reception and the time was around 3 a.m. He describes what happened:

I suddenly heard a gentle thud and looked up to discover one of the candles had apparently fallen from the mantelpiece and was lying on the floor in the middle of the reception area. It did not seem logical to me, to land where it did; it should have been in the well of the fireplace itself.

But there was more to come:

I was suddenly distracted again by the movement on the mantlepiece. Looking up I saw the candle rise up a few inches above the shelf, move slightly to the right and then float out across the reception area towards me and plonk itself down again on the floor from where I had previously picked it up.

He doggedly returned the candle to its rightful place on the mantelpiece. This time it stayed put. Michael describes the effect on his own body perhaps created by these ghostly visitors. He says, while working in the library in the dead of night:

I have, on at least two occasions, experienced a very sudden, chilling and dramatic change in the surrounding atmosphere. I could feel my body temperature falling at an alarming rate to the point I thought I was experiencing the onset of a heart attack or something similar. The effect was quite dramatic enough to force me to abandon what I was doing and to retreat to the hotel kitchen where I was able to get some heat back into me by standing next to the ovens. On both occasions this experience occurred in exactly the same location within the library which, along with the rest of the building, is centrally heated.

On another occasion, when he was vacuuming the library, the vacuum cleaner suddenly switched itself on and off, on and off – unaided by any human hand – four or five times. He could actually see the switches moving.

But what could Michael find in the history of the building? The night manager delved deep into family records. He discovered that the library is said to be haunted by a priest who, in his lifetime, was overly fond of practical jokes.

As set out earlier, the Shirley family owned Ettington for more than 1,000 years and many hotel guests have seen the ghosts of the Shirley children. They were tragically drowned in the nineteenth century, in the River Stour, which runs through the estate. The kids' favourite spot in the hotel seems to be the Stour corridor and the Stour Suite. Guests have phoned down to report the shrill voices of children, the shrieks and the rough and tumble of play. But, on more than one occasion, after an exhaustive search, no children were found and none were registered as being guests of the hotel.

Michael continues his amazing ghostly experiences with the supernatural. It was about 3 a.m. one night when he made himself a cup of tea.

I had hardly sat down, when I heard the voice of a young girl calling out 'Mama, Mama!' It came from the Stour corridor. I concluded that some child had woken up in the night and wandered out of her room looking for her parents' bedroom. But there was no child to be seen nor registered at the hotel. A week later, they were at it again: It was the childish voice of a boy calling out 'Michael, Michael!'

It was the same story as before. No children were registered at the hotel. No children anywhere. [Hearing one's name being called is not unknown at haunted locations.]

A recent ghost was referred to as the Grey Lady. She was possibly a former mistress of the house, or perhaps a governess to the Shirley children. For once, Michael had no dealings with her. Instead, she made an appearance to two guests at the hotel. They had been woken twice during the night by 'an old lady in Victorian style dress who stood resolutely at the end of the bed.' It was all too much for them. Despite it being 2 a.m., they hurriedly left the hotel.

The night manager continues. He describes his most dramatic ghostly encounter with a stranger and his dog. Like many of his other middle-of-the-night contacts, it occurred at about 3 a.m:

Suddenly and unexpectedly, a dog walked into view through a doorway on my left and proceeded to walk across the reception towards the library. The dog looked like a lurcher or a young Irish wolfhound... a man also walked through the doorway following the dog as it headed towards the library. The man wore a tweed jacket, riding breeches and boots. Stepping forward, I said, 'Can I help you?' There was no response or even the faintest acknowledgement of my presence. He swept past me and disappeared into the library. But there was no one there – neither man nor beast.

Michael investigated further. The last member of the Shirley family to reside at Ettington was Sewallis Edward Shirley, who died in 1912. Furthermore, he was founder of the Kennel Club of Great Britain. Could this be the relationship?

Michael now tells the story of a blind nineteenth century harpist who just might have been playing the haunting music he heard emanating from the Great

Drawing Room. Like the good detective he is, Michael checked to see if any of the hotel music systems were on. They were off. He writes: 'I recently discovered that a famous Irish harpist called Patrick Byrne lived as a guest of the Shirley family at Ettington.' He was born in 1774 into a tenant family living on the Shirley estate at Lough Fea in County Monaghan, in Ireland.

He became a celebrity, travelled through England, Ireland, and Scotland and eventually was honoured as Royal Harpist to his Royal Highness, Prince Albert. When he died in 1863 he left his harp to the Shirley family. Michael aches to make the connection – Irish harpist brings music back to Ettington. Well, it just might be, Michael concludes.

The retired night manager describes another incident that happened when he was least expecting it. Suddenly, all the bolts on all the doors shot back simultaneously. He wrote that outside, the night was pitch black. 'I could hear the hooting of owls and the strange barking calls of the munjac deer echoed eerily into the room from the surrounding woodlands.'

And when you think you have covered all the supernatural instances, you come across one more. Michael remembered a man preparing for a conference one evening, who rushed down to reception exclaiming, 'I'm not going back up there alone.' He had suddenly been grabbed by the shoulders and spun round by an invisible force. 'I came up and stayed with him,' Michael said. 'There's a lot of staff who won't come up into the Long Gallery in the evening. But I've not found anything threatening.'

It is a simple question. Does Michael believe in ghosts? To a man who's looked so many phantoms in the eye, isn't the answer quite obvious? Well, Michael, who has a degree in history and another in psychology, has his own theory, which, in some ways, is similar to Andrew's. He suggests that a place may 'record' certain past incidents, both audio and visual, and replay them in the future. After all, we can record sound and pictures in many ways – tapes, CDs, DVDs and so on. Maybe it's possible for this to occur naturally, for a place to record incidents from the past.

He suggests that the energy expended during certain events lingers and can be picked up by some very sensitive people. He himself suffers from a particularly high static electricity charge in his own body and is unable to wear a wrist watch as it just stops dead. Andrew, remember, suffered from temple epilepsy that also made him extraordinarily sensitive to some things.   This has been one of the most detailed accounts of haunting that I have ever come across. In the space of five years, Michael describes some fifteen ghosts or ghostly manifestations; in most of them he has been personally involved in the haunting or he has been somewhere close to the action. But he never went looking for ghosts. It happened to him when he was least expecting them – doing something else entirely – going through papers, reading and so on. This is really an incredible number. Most ghost-hunters who go looking for ghosts never find them. Andrew in a lifetime saw only four.

Back in 1980, Andrew discovered four ghosts in what was then the Ettington Park Country Club. He writes of inexplicable footsteps walking along an empty corridor in the early hours, invisible material stroked over the face of a guest in the bedroom, and the phantom of a lady in white. The lady, wearing a long gown, and known as Lady Emma, has been seen walking along the cloister-like terrace beside the arched entrance. Andrew was told she glided along the hallway and when she reached the wall 'it seemed as if she just melted into it.'

With the help of Michael Kenny, this has been an extraordinary adventure. In my mind, there seems little doubt that I should agree with the AA. This really must be the most haunted hotel in Britain. (If you don't agree, write to the publisher).

ETTINGTON PARK HOTEL
STRATFORD-ON-AVON, WARWICKSHIRE, CU37 8BU.
TEL: 01789 450123.
OPEN TO THE PUBLIC AT APPROPRIATE HOURS

THIRTY-ONE

West Midlands

DUDLEY CASTLE

So that's what little ghosts are made of

'Ghosts are only images that have been recorded in history and are [now] being played back. We cannot interact with them. It's a matter of learning to read the signals,' Dudley Castle's Simon Duarte said. 'That is the mantra. It's what the guides to this eleventh century edifice always tell their visitors.' Andrew would probably agree (though he would have added a few thoughts of his own).

Dudley Castle began conducting ghost tours back in the early 1980s, and over the past thirty years or so has picked up a number of sightings, from both professional mediums and members of the public. If three people independently see the same ghost, then, it's said, there is a good chance it's genuine.

We'll start with what the castle calls the 'infamous' Grey lady. Quite a number of haunted places in the UK seem to have their own Grey Lady; why this is I have yet to discover. Certainly the Grey Lady at Dudley Castle seems to do very little: she 'haunts' the castle itself and walks through the castle grounds.

It seems to me that the Grey Lady here is Dorothy Baumont, wife to the second-in-command of the Royalist forces (Her husband, Lt John Beaumont, saw action in the mid-seventeenth-century Civil War at the castle). She is believed to have given birth to a child in September 1645, but the baby died soon afterwards. She died herself in the following April 1646 and has forever afterwards been searching for her 'lost' child. If you see her, that is what she is doing. Say nothing.

But what of the Grey Lady, or for that matter, the White Lady, who seems to crop up in every second haunting? Well, in his *Haunted Brighton*, Alan Murdie has some interesting things to say, in which he draws data from John Rackham's *Brighton Ghosts and Hove Hauntings*.

There is apparently a pattern of individual staff seeing a White Lady at night – or at least in the dark. Don't look for the identity of the lady; you won't find one. Unless of course you'd like to imagine her as one of the many mistresses of George IV, who is very closely associated with Brighton. Some ghost-hunters now think the ghost represents simply nobody. There is a lot more on the subject in Alan's most interesting book.

Getting back to Dudley Castle and its hauntings, another place where ghost activity has been spotted is in the kitchen area. In one doorway above the kitchen, the ghost of a beautiful woman in a full-length ball gown is often seen. No-one is sure of her identity but she is thought to be a family member of the lords of Dudley. Visitors complain that the lady is looking down on them. This is nonsense, says Simon. As he said earlier, ghosts simply don't react. This ghost 'eventually turns round and walks back through the doorway and disappears.'

The next ghost is said to be that of King Charles I, a friend of that long-ago Earl of Dudley, William Humbleward. Apparently the King visited the castle ten days before his capture at Worcester. His ghost has been seen walking through a doorway or through one of the castle's fireplaces, where he then disappears.

There are a number of ghosts associated with the castle keep. A Civil War soldier often patrols the motte on which the keep actually stands. There are two cannons captured from the Russians during the Crimean War which were presented to the town of Dudley; this was a gift of thanks to the local yeomanry who helped win the peace. Ghosts of Russian soldiers are often seen round about the (Russian) cannons as though they were on active service.

Dudley Castle. (courtesy of Simon Duarte, Dudley Castle Education Department)

Russian ghosts guard the Russian cannons.

A so-called witch has been seen hanging from the battlements. This was the cruel punishment of any woman judged to be a witch. She could have been a simpleton, or the object of a grudge; almost any accusation may have succeeded in branding a woman as a witch. One such witch associated with the castle was Margaret de Sutton. Because she produced some kinds of herbal medicine, she was accused of practising witchcraft and – with no trial – simply hung over the battlements of the keep. By some kind of cock-eyed thinking, her death proved she was innocent.

The undercroft (above ground cellar) of many castles is often a refuge for ghosts; and so it is in Dudley Castle. John Dudley, the most famous and powerful of the Earls of Dudley, still walks the corridors here. He's a bit of a cheeky ghost as he once shouted into a nervous woman's ear, 'Get Out!'

Many people perished in a fire here in July 1740 and it is thought their spirits still inhabit the place. Up until 1539, 'black monks' regularly visited the castle from the nearby priory and their presence is often felt in the undercroft. One possible ghostly manifestation from these monks is an unknown force that has compelled people there to sit in a prayer-like posture.

The Chequerboard Room is haunted by a little girl that a medium has identified as Ellie. She is believed to be seven years old with blonde hair. Young children have often been attracted to Ellie. If Ellie stands immediately in front of a child, facing her, nobody else in the room can see her. In this posture, she has been offered toys, food, and milk. Ellie has also been known to run around people playing ring-a-ring-roses, a popular game since the Tudor period.

The final section of the undercroft, not part of the museum, under the old family chapel, is the crypt. This was the torture chamber of the castle where enemies of the duke could expect a grisly end.

The fireplace in the crypt has been known to glow abnormally brightly, with a black mist moving across it. It is thought that the room has been the springboard of a poltergeist. A young girl [not identified] going through puberty is suspected of being the source for the throwing of stones and other missiles.

The castle has an impressive number of ghosts today and it is interesting to see what Andrew made of it all back in 1973. He seems to have found little of the paranormal then. He writes of 'two elderly people dressed in seventeenth-century clothes. They appear to walk arm-in-arm up to the twelfth-century gatehouse and vanish.' Numerous odd sounds were heard as well as the clash of what could be sword blades.

Andrew gives a detailed history of the castle, saying that it was one of the few castles mentioned in the Domesday Book of 1086. He also tells us that the castle is of course linked with the busy Dudley Zoological Society – as it is today.

As I write this, Queen Elizabeth II is braving a royal tour of the United States, with the provision of several banquets, acres of red carpet and tables loaded with silver. But whatever preparations are being made now, they fade into insignificance when compared with the visit of the former Queen Elizabeth I to Dudley Castle in 1575. A withdrawing room was hastily erected, as well as a warden's tower and an angle tower. The amount of food was prodigious. But whispers in dark corners predicted that the preparations could serve as well for the visit of Mary Queen of Scots – whom Elizabeth eventually had executed.

Few buildings in the UK can boast such a variety of ghosties. Do see if you can manage a visit – it's worth every shriek.

DUDLEY CASTLE
DUDLEY CASTLE, DUDLEY ZOOLOGICAL GARDENS,
2 THE BROADWAY, DUDLEY, WEST MIDLANDS, DY1 4QB.
TEL: 01384 215301.
OPEN TO THE PUBLIC DURING ZOO HOURS

THIRTY-TWO

West Sussex

THE LION HOTEL

A secret haunting 'till morning

They might leave in a hurry. This is a hotel so sinister that the landlord will not divulge its real haunting until the guests have stayed the night. Just in case they do a runner.

Well, the landlord, Graham Godwyn, is a pragmatist. There are reports by ordinary guests and many pages written by ghost-hunters, and some say parts of the hotel are evil. That might be something you'd keep mum about till the bill has been paid. You can see Graham's point, can't you?

The Lion Hotel has a vast history going back earlier than 1407, when we know some building work was carried out. It was on a site mentioned in the *Domesday Book*. Some four centuries later, in the eighteenth and early nineteenth centuries, the whole area of Nyetimber, Pagham, and Selsey was frequented by smugglers. There are many accounts of tubs of brandy being run ashore and secreted away in various properties. There seems little doubt that the Lion was once a smugglers' haunt. There is even a 'spy window' on the top floor, facing towards Chichester – from where the customs men usually came.

There have been many changes over the years. There is said to be a priest hole behind the panels of one of the inglenooks (which the present landlord has been unable to find) and a secret tunnel, now filled in, which used to lead to Barton Manor. There is also supposed to be a secret panel in one of the bedrooms but nobody seems to know to where it leads.

The present landlord took over the property in May 2003. He is pleased to show us what a haunted hotel is really like. Since he obtained the property, he has had this extraordinary complaint about room two. In the middle of the night the wife heard a woman singing. Yes, singing. But as soon as she woke her slumbering husband, the singing stopped.

But the next story is even stranger. On two separate occasions, in different bedrooms, two guests have been wakened by something pulling an arm, presumably to get them out of bed. Neither victim could remember the time when the arm pull really happened but they were too frightened to stay in that bedroom again.

In September 2004, with the aid of a medium, a number of hotel guests organised a ghost-hunt. The medium 'sensed' a woman standing by the window in room two as well as a 'sinister' character in the bar area (not further described). At this point, however, the medium looked exceedingly ill at ease. 'Nothing', he said, 'nothing' would make him stay. He was scared and uncomfortable. He then said something quite extraordinary. Somebody was 'imprisoning the woman upstairs'. The true meaning of this was never discovered.

Mr Godwyn tried to make sense of what he had heard and made a visit to the local library. Here he found a reference to his hotel where the haunting was done by 'a lady in a blue or grey dress'. She wore 'a radiant smile'

That's the kind of happy ghost that the landlord likes to meet.

THE LION HOTEL
NYETIMBER, PAGHAM, BOGNOR REGIS, WEST SUSSEX.
TEL: 01243 262149
OPEN TO THE PUBLIC AT THE APPROPRIATE TIMES.

THIRTY-THREE

Wiltshire

KING & QUEEN INN

Another monk, but this one's lost his head

Once upon a time, a monk was murdered here – taken out of the building and strung up for getting a local girl into trouble. That's mob-justice. Lynch law. Or was he perhaps judicially killed, after a proper law court? (This 500-year-old building once housed a courthouse). Nobody seems to know for sure, but the regulars have their own ideas.

There are stories of past landlords insuring against a customer dying of fright – after coming face to face with the apparitions. One publican told the story about his two alsatians, savage beasts, that will protect their master to the death: but one day they were confronted by something almost invisible to their master but plain for them to see. And they didn't like what they plainly saw.

The two dogs, out in the cobble-stoned inn yard, started howling. Quite unlike their usual barking. When their owner went outside to see, instead of rushing to him as they usually did, the dogs were crouching down, silent, side by side, their tails sticking out, their hair bristling. When the landlord looked in the direction the dogs were staring at, he saw, just for an instant, for a fleeting moment, the dwarf-like figure of a monk – but without its head. After a split-second, the figure glided through the wall. The dogs became silent except for a few perfunctory barks, and returned to their snoring and snapping at insects.

There are still plenty of spooky things going on at the King & Queen. Lights flicker, shadows appear from nowhere. And sometimes there are sudden drops in temperature. These things, more than anything, attract ghost-hunters to this inn.

Mr Champ, twenty-seven, who lives in the pub, said his former scepticism over ghosts and ghouls is starting to fade. He puts this down to a number of 'incidents,' convincing evidence that ghosts are real. He also says that he has heard lots of stories about a monk haunting the pub which are obviously also convincing. Mr Champ said, 'I don't think it's time for an exorcist, but it is intriguing. I am the most sceptical man in the world but with the King & Queen I know there is something there.'

Regulars were discussing the chap who went to use the outside loo, and returned white as a sheet. He remained tight-lipped about what happened and said he was keeping mum about the experience. He would only say that he had seen an apparition.

Another regular admitted that he didn't believe a thing but nevertheless could feel just a little nervous on the darkest nights. The King & Queen is an old pub, he said, 'with cracks, bangs, and groans everywhere. Peripherally, you are aware of dark shadows. And that, added to the stories you hear, makes you start to think.'

The King & Queen attracts ghost-hunters from all over the world, all of whom have come to see the horrors (much exaggerated). It might have tempted another two overseas tourists who, last month, begged to be allowed to stay in a particular room to catch sight of the headless monk.

Another local said: 'This pub was an old coaching inn and yet more anecdotal evidence indicates that a monk was once hung in the alley for stealing a loaf of bread. I am sure that being a coaching inn there would have been a lot of unscrupulous people coming through these doors.' Finally, the remarks of another local: 'There is so much history here. The attic has not been touched for 150 years and there are still wooden slats on the ceiling.'

Andrew, writing in 1973, says that the pub, some 500 yeas old, is on the site of an old monastery. There is, Andrew said, supposed to be a tunnel from the pub to the nearby church, and it was from this tunnel that the phantoms came. The description of the phantoms was that they were 'crouched like hunchbacks.'

He also found that a ghost had been seen in Pentlands Lane, not far from the King & Queen. This ghost appeared to a group of teenagers and also to a van driver. The ghost was described as shining white and had also been seen on a nearby field.

KING & QUEEN INN
15 HIGH STREET, HIGHWORTH, WILTSHIRE, SN6 7AG,
TEL: 01793 762293
OPEN TO THE PUBLIC AT THE APPROPRIATE TIMES

LONGLEAT

The beautiful ghost

It was jealousy that did it. Plain old-fashioned jealousy: it caused a death and precipitated a ghost. And involved a murder.

Well, to begin at the beginning; in the late eighteenth century, Longleat – that massive splendid sixteenth century pile – was to have a new bride. Louise Carteret, of an impeccable background, was not only strikingly beautiful, it was said she also had an angelic disposition. The man she was to marry, Thomas, the second Viscount Weymouth, on the other hand, was ill-tempered, unpredictable and inclined to jealous rages.

Following the custom of the rich and famous, Louise brought her staff with her – those she knew and loved. Among these trusty servants was a particularly good looking footman. And therein lies the plot. For no apparent reason, Weymouth thought his wife was being unfaithful with the handsome footman. Was there really anything going on? The general consensus is that there was nothing improper. Louise was as innocent as Desdemona.

But from here the story breaks into several strands. In one version, Weymouth found the footman in an upstairs corridor close to Lady Louise's bedroom. Ignoring the servant's protestations of innocence, the viscount drew his sword and after a violent fight, ran the unfortunate footman through with his sword.

There's yet a further story. In this version, a Longleat lackey suggested to his master that the footman knew more of Louise than was proper; at this the master flew into a furious jealous rage. He and other staff waited outside the Old Library and when the victim appeared, threw him down the spiral staircase that led to the next floor down. The fall broke his neck and caused almost instant death.

Andrew, writing in 1980, comes up with yet another story in his brief entry. He is far more critical when he writes about Louisa. According to Andrew, the Viscount discovered the two together as lovers and challenged the footman to a duel (it would have been a rare eighteenth century footman who was adept with a sword). The conclusion, however, was the same. The servant was run through with a sword. Andrew adds that the ghost, always wearing a green dress, haunts 'the Green Lady's walk'.

As the realization dawned that (after whatever version) a murder investigation was imminent, which would involve the Viscount, it was agreed something must be done. And done now. One assumes that the staff were loyal to their master and sworn to secrecy. Weymouth directs that the corpse be taken down to the cellar and buried under the flagstones. A plot had then to be hatched to explain away the footman's sudden disappearance. The story was put out that the footman had simply gone away – something that Louisa never believed.

Louisa died soon after this affair, and it is believed that her ghost can be seen vainly searching the upstairs rooms for her faithful footman in the hope that he may have been imprisoned there against his will.

Shortly after Louisa's death, the second Viscount moved out of Longleat altogether, to live in the village of Horningsham (quite near to Longleat) instead. Why? Well, there were whispers. Was he terrified of running into Louisa as she drifted through the old rooms on the upper floors of Longleat after dark – forever looking for her murdered footman? They just could have been right. As we have written several times in the rest of this book, a ghost can be scary – particularly perhaps if you are guilty of its murder!

There is an interesting postscript to this story that the present Viscount says himself. Here it is:

When my grandfather, the fifth Marquess, introduced central heating for the first time to Longleat, soon after the turn of the [twentieth] century, the floor in the basement had to be lowered in order to take the new boiler. And, on digging down beneath the flagstones, a body was discovered – in a bad state of decay, but with crumbling raiment and boots that could be dated as of a style worn in the reign of Queen Anne (1702-1714). Even at the belated date of the Edwardian era, when these human remains were unearthed, my grandfather was anxious to avoid too serious a police investigation. So everything that had not completely crumbled into dust was scooped up into a hatbox and buried in the local church cemetery (by an odd coincidence) where the remains of the second Viscount had long lain uneasily to rest.

There are other Longleat ghosts to investigate and there is no denying this magnificent Tudor mansion has many ways to tempt you with its stately rooms, gardens and safari park. It's set within 900 acres, landscaped by Capability Brown, part of it given to lions, tigers and giraffe.

But be wary gliding through those upstairs rooms…

LONGLEAT
WARMINSTER, WILTSHIRE. BA12 7NW.
TEL: 01985 844400
OPEN AT THE APPROPRIATE TIMES
OPEN TO GHOSTS AT ANY TIME

THIRTY-FOUR

Yorkshire

YORK THEATRE ROYAL

The see-through lady and walled-up nuns

York Theatre Royal has had its fair share of ghosts and those used to their comings and goings can be quite sanguine about the whole thing. But this doesn't apply to the ordinary theatregoer who may well go into some kind of shock seeing ghosts suddenly appear and disappear. The following stories took place a couple of years ago at the York Theatre Royal. The first happened during a matinee performance of the pantomime.

In the interval a lady came up to the box office to ask if there was a paid-up member of the audience sitting directly in front of her. (All seats were allocated from a plan). She thought she might be taken for a fool but she had to tell someone.

While watching the show from the upper circle she noticed a lady sitting a few rows in front of her and initially she thought nothing of it. It was only when she realized that she was able to see right through the lady to the other side that panic seized her. Gradually, before her eyes, the transparent lady in front disappeared.

But that wasn't the only journey into the supernatural experienced by the theatre. Katy Nelson, PA to the directors, told me that she and another member of staff were locking up one night with the certainty that they were not alone. Then they heard it, as clear as daylight, the clatter, clatter, clatter of footsteps. They were heading from the direction of the dressing rooms. Katy heard the door leading to the stage open and shut. The two girls made a thorough search of the stage and the surrounding area. They called, they yelled. Is anyone there? Nobody was there; at least that was what they concluded. They looked at each other – and fled.

Well, that takes care of recent hauntings. We'll now look at some of the spooks Andrew discovered some thirty years ago. He introduces us to the unpleasant custom of immurement, by which a monk or nun would agree to be virtually walled up in a small cell for life. The face was quite open so that food would be passed in and empty containers and other things passed out. For some reason, Andrew says, females rather than males seemed to take greater 'delight' in being housed in this ghastly living tomb.

The colour of the robes, grey or white, often provide an indication as to the status of the wearer, a lay sister or accredited nun, or the order to which they belonged. Thus the so-named Grey Lady of the Theatre Royal, which opened in 1740, is actually associated not with the stage, but with the ruins of the St Leonards Hospital which now forms part of the theatre. The crypt of the original hospital has been turned into a social centre and club room for the theatre.

St Leonards Hospital was one of the first religious foundations devoted to the care of the sick. And one assumes it was also used, as was the custom, for housing both monks and nuns. There is an old legend that monks and nuns could be walled up completely, quite against their will, when the punishment was death. Recent research, however has gone strongly against this and now classifies it as an old wives tale with no evidence to back up the claim.

But apparitions of ghosts suggest that there was a strong link with a religious order. In just one example out of many, a former actress, Mrs Marjorie Rowland, relates that, while standing at the back of the circle, she saw the figure of a nun, dressed in grey with a white coif, leaning over the edge of the stage box. The description seems to suggest that the ghost was that of a novice who had not qualified for full sisterhood. There are many more examples.

And through it all, the show goes on.

YORK THEATRE ROYAL
ST LEONARDS PLACE, YORK, NORTH YORKSHIRE, YO1 7HD.
TEL: 01904 658162.
OPEN AT THE APPROPRIATE TIMES

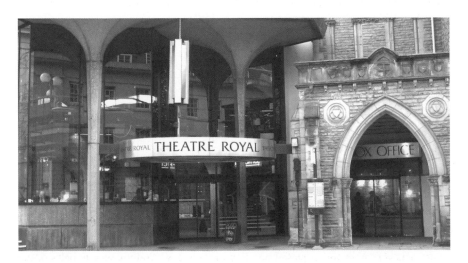

If there's somebody in your seat, check first it isn't a ghost (they don't pay for their seats).

Index